FREE WILL and DETERMINISM

FREE WILL and DETERMINISM

A DIALOGUE

CLIFFORD WILLIAMS

HACKETT PUBLISHING COMPANY
Indianapolis • Cambridge

Cover design by Richard L. Listenberger
Interior design by James N. Rogers
Printed in the United States of America

12 11 10 9 99

For further information, please address
Hackett Publishing Company, Inc.
Box 44937, Indianapolis, Indiana 46244-0937

Library of Congress Cataloging in Publication Data

Williams, Clifford, 1943–
Free will and determinism: A Dialogue.

Bibliography: p.
Includes index.
1. Free will and determinism. I. Title.
BJ1460.W54 123 79-24164
ISBN 0–915144–78–6
ISBN 0–915144–77–8 pbk.

The paper used in this publication meets the minimum requirements of American National Standard for Information Sciences—Permanence of Paper for Printed Library Materials, ANSI Z39.48-1984.

Contents

Preface

The aim of this book is to present the main features of the problem of free will and determinism via a dialogue that is clear, readable and interesting. I have attempted to make the dialogue suitable for persons who have had little or no background in philosophy.

The participants in the dialogue are Daniel, who is a determinist; Frederick, who is a free-willist; and Carolyn, who is a compatibilist. Each participant is of equal status—no one is presented as representing the correct viewpoint. The reader can remember more easily which position each participant holds by noting that the first letter of each of their names is the same as the first letter of the position that each holds.

The reader's attention is drawn to the abstract that begins on page 59. It summarizes the entire dialogue, section by section, and may be of some benefit to those wishing to review the structure of the ideas presented in the dialogue.

A list of questions for each section appears at the end of the dialogue.

I would like to thank the following persons for the suggestions they made on various parts of the book: William Carrington, Arthur F. Holmes, George G. Lavere, Robert McLaughlin, John R. Perry, and David White. I want especially to thank my wife Linda for making numerous helpful comments on the entire manuscript. I am also grateful to St. John Fisher College for granting me a sabbatical for Spring, 1977, during which a portion of the dialogue was written.

Clifford Williams

FREE WILL and DETERMINISM
A Dialogue

Participants:

FREDERICK: Free-willist
DANIEL: Determinist
CAROLYN: Compatibilist

INTRODUCTORY REMARKS

FREDERICK: Here comes Carolyn. Maybe she can tell us what she thinks about the case.

DANIEL: Hello, Carolyn.

CAROLYN: Hello, Daniel. Hi, Frederick.

FREDERICK: Daniel and I were talking about the Leopold and Loeb murder trial.

CAROLYN: Was that the trial at which Clarence Darrow tried to persuade the judge that the defendants should not be hanged for murdering a little boy?

FREDERICK: Yes. The trial made headlines all over the country. Nathan Leopold and Richard Loeb were only eighteen years old at the time, and their parents were well known throughout Chicago where they lived.

CAROLYN: Why did Leopold and Loeb kill the little boy?

FREDERICK: They wanted to commit the perfect crime.

CAROLYN: Is that all?

FREDERICK: Yes. They went to a school just as the children were leaving, picked up a youngster whom they happened to know, drove around for awhile, and then hit him on the head with a chisel, so that he bled to death right in the car. After that, they stuffed his body into a culvert in some out-of-the-way locality.

CAROLYN: How ghastly!

FREDERICK: I agree. Maybe that's why the newspapers played it up so big.

CAROLYN: What was Darrow's strategy at the trial?

FREDERICK: Darrow argued that the judge should have compassion on the two young murderers, because what they did was the product of causes over which they had no control. Let me read to you what he actually said. "I do not know what it was that made these boys do this mad act, but I do know there is a reason for it. I know they did not beget themselves. I know that any one of an infinite number of causes reaching back to the beginning might be working out in these boys' minds, whom you are asked to hang in malice and in hatred and injustice, because someone in the past has sinned against them."

CAROLYN: That certainly is a bold strategy for a defense attorney to use!

FREDERICK: Yes it is. Listen to what he goes on to say. "Nature is strong and she is pitiless. She works in her own mysterious way, and we are her victims. We have not much to do with it ourselves. Nature takes this job in hand, and we play our parts."

CAROLYN: Was the judge persuaded to reduce Leopold and Loeb's punishment?

FREDERICK: Yes, he must have been, because he sentenced them to life imprisonment, even though he was under great pressure from the public to sentence them to death.

CAROLYN: What do you think about Darrow's strategy?

FREDERICK: I think it is absurd, because it is based on the false belief that everything we do is determined. If that were true, then the two murderers could not have acted freely, which is obviously false.

DANIEL: I would say that Clarence Darrow is right in believing that everything we do is determined. If that means that the two murderers did not act freely, then that is what we should believe.

FREDERICK: What would you say about this case, Carolyn?

CAROLYN: I think Darrow is right in believing that everything we do is caused by previous happenings. But I also think that we are free and morally responsible for what we do.

FREDERICK: That sounds contradictory to me. If it was determined that Leopold and Loeb would kill the little boy, I don't see how they could have done it freely.

DANIEL: Why don't we discuss the whole issue of free will and determinism? Maybe we can resolve our disagreements.

FREDERICK: That's a good idea. Would you like to stay, Carolyn?

CAROLYN: Yes, I would be glad to. I don't think, however, that the issue should be put solely in terms of free will *or* determinism.

FREDERICK: How do you think it should be put?

CAROLYN: I would say that there are three main questions: One, do people have free will? Two, is determinism true? And three, are free will and determinism compatible?

FREDERICK: My answers to those questions are that people have free will, that free will and determinism are incompatible, and, therefore, that determinism is false.

DANIEL: My reasoning is just the opposite. Since determinism is true, people have no free will.

CAROLYN: I agree with you, Frederick, that people have freedom, and with you Daniel, that determinism is true, but I don't think that the two conflict.

DETERMINISM

FREDERICK: Perhaps we should define "determinism" before we start discussing our positions.

CAROLYN: That's a good idea. My definition of "determinism" is, "Everything that happens is caused to happen." In contemporary philosophical jargon, this is the same as saying that every event has a cause. That includes everything we ever do, think or say.

FREDERICK: Why do you define it that way and not as "People have no control over anything they do"?

CAROLYN: Because the question of whether or not we have control over anything we do is different from the question of whether or not everything we do is caused. And each of these two questions is different from the question of whether we can have control over anything we do *even if* everything we do is caused. That's why I said before that there are *three* main questions and not just two: One, Do we have control over anything we do? Two, Is everything we do caused? And three, Can we have control over what we do even if everything we do is caused? We can discuss these three questions separately, so we can give three different names to their answers—"free will" if we answer "Yes" to the first; "determinism" if we answer "Yes" to the second; and "compatibilism" if we answer "Yes" to the third.

DANIEL: Don't people usually think of determinism as saying

that people have no free will?

CAROLYN: Yes, people probably do think of determinism in that way. But I think that what determinism *says* should be clearly distinguished from what it may or may not *entail*. It says only that everything that happens is caused. Whether or not it entails that we have no free will is a different question altogether.

FREDERICK: You're saying that we should define "determinism" in a relatively neutral way, such as "Everything that happens has a cause," and talk first about whether this claim is true, and then about whether it entails that we have no free will, right?

CAROLYN: Right.

FREDERICK: That sounds like a good procedure.

DANIEL: I'll start by giving my reason for believing that everything that happens has a cause. I think this is true because of the enormous amount of happenings for which we have found causes. Both in daily life and in science we come across countless cases of caused happenings.

FREDERICK: Can you give some examples?

DANIEL: Yes. Wind causes trees to bend. Rain causes plants to grow. Friction causes heat.

FREDERICK: Can you give examples involving people?

DANIEL: Yes. Hunger causes people to eat. Peer pressure causes people to conform. Stress causes people to become tense. And so on. There are so many instances of what we do being caused that one cannot escape the conclusion that everything we do is caused.

CAROLYN: I agree.

DANIEL: And the extraordinary success of science in finding explanations makes it almost impossible to doubt determinism. Biology tells us that heredity determines what kind of persons we will be. Sociology tells us that environmental factors determine much of what we do. Psychology tells us that what we become as adults is influenced largely by what happens to us when we are young children. Psychiatry tells us that our conscious desires are products of unconscious motives. Neurology tells us that what we do is caused by electrical-chemical happenings in our brains. And all of them together tell us that everything we do, say, want or think is produced entirely by previous occurrences.

FREDERICK: How would you explain the murder committed by Leopold and Loeb?

DANIEL: According to the psychiatrist who examined them, they were emotionally ill. One of them was paranoic and had intense nervous energy; the other was manic-depressive and had as a personal philosophy the gratification of his own desires. Given these factors, we can see what triggered their outburst of murderous passion.

FREDERICK: How would you explain an everyday occurrence, such as my buying a mystery novel?

DANIEL: Based on what I know about you, I would say that your delight in reading suspense stories and your knowing that you will have some free time cause you to make the purchase.

CAROLYN: I like what you have been saying, Daniel. I think determinism is true for the same reason you do. Would you mind if I stated that reason in a different way?

DANIEL: No, go ahead.

CAROLYN: I want to link up your statement about finding causes with a description of what exactly it is for a happening to have a cause.

DANIEL: Okay.

CAROLYN: If something that happens is caused to happen, then it could have been different in the way it happened only if something just prior to it were different. But if something that happens has *no* cause, then it could have been different in the way it happened *even if* everything just prior to it were exactly the same. That means that determinism would not be correct *if*, whenever we found differences in the way things usually happen, we *also* found that the prior conditions were exactly the same. But we never do find this. What we find is that whenever there are differences in the way things usually happen, there are also differences in the prior conditions. The only fair conclusion, I think, is that determinism is true.

FREDERICK: Could you illustrate that with an example?

CAROLYN: Yes. Suppose a strong gust of wind hits the tree in my front yard but does not knock it down. And suppose that later another strong gust of wind hits the tree and does knock it down. We would naturally think that the conditions prior to the tree's falling down were different from what they were when the wind hit the tree the first time.

Perhaps the wind was stronger the second time, or perhaps it hit the tree from a different direction. The reason we would think this is that we naturally think that the wind caused the tree to fall over the second time. We would say that the tree's falling over has no cause only if we found that the initial conditions each time were exactly the same. But in a case like this, we invariably find some difference in the initial conditions.

FREDERICK: Do you think the same can be said about what people do?

CAROLYN: Yes. Suppose one person reacts with great anger to personal insults, whereas another person reacts with calmness and equanimity. When we look into their characters, we find differences that account for the different ways they react. We don't find that their genetic inheritance and social and family environment are exactly the same. But only if we did find this could we say that determinism is false.

FREDERICK: What would you say about identical twins who are brought up in the same family, yet who grow up to have different personalities? That seems to me to be a case in which the initial conditions are the same but the outcomes are different.

CAROLYN: If you could show me a case where identical twins grew up in exactly the same environment yet turned out to be different, then I would admit that determinism is false. But showing that two children grew up in exactly the same environment seems impossible. There are vast differences in the way children are treated and in what they experience. These differences can lead to still further differences, and so produce different personalities.

DANIEL: I would be interested in hearing your reactions to our argument for determinism, Frederick.

FREDERICK: Well, as I have already said, I don't think determinism is true. So, naturally, I disagree with your argument for it.

DANIEL: What do you think is wrong with our argument?

FREDERICK: Two things. In the first place, I don't think it shows that *everything* we do is determined. And in the second place, it seems to me to ignore the fact that there is concrete evidence against determinism.

DANIEL: Could you explain each of those points?

FREDERICK: Yes. I'll start with the first one. Even though you two are right in saying that science and everyday experience show that much of what we do is determined, I don't think there is enough evidence to show that everything is. There are, after all, many happenings for which we don't know the causes. And there are many areas of human behavior that scientists haven't investigated yet. So I don't see how you can claim that *all* of what we do is caused.

DANIEL: Carolyn and I aren't saying that people actually have discovered the causes of every happening. What we are saying is that it is legitimate to *infer* that everything we do is determined from the fact that much of what we do is determined. In daily life, we frequently make this kind of inference. For instance, we infer that all of the grass in the world is green after seeing only some of the world's grass. We infer that all heavy objects fall on the basis of seeing only a small number of heavy objects fall. If you think these inferences are valid, then you should believe that determinism is true on the basis of the evidence that science and everyday experience provide.

FREDERICK: No, I don't think I should, because the percentage of the world's events we have observed is much smaller than the percentage of grass and falling objects we have observed. In the case of the grass and falling objects, we may have seen as much as five or ten percent, but when it comes to the total number of events in the world, we can scarcely have observed more than one-millionth of one-millionth of one percent. In view of this fact, isn't it rather presumptuous to say that every single event is caused?

DANIEL: No, it's not presumptuous, because over the past several centuries, scientists have discovered the causes of enormous numbers of occurrences. Surely, that is a good reason for believing in determinism.

FREDERICK: Compared to what scientists knew centuries ago, we do, indeed, have a great deal of knowledge. But compared to what could be known, we have very little. And even the knowledge scientists do have about people is general and imprecise. It leaves plenty of room for free and uncaused actions. For example, you said earlier that peer pressure causes people to conform. But that's not always so. There are plenty of exceptions. And there are exceptions to almost every other causal explanation of people's behavior.

DANIEL: That may be true, but science has progressed to the point where many of the exceptions can themselves be explained. If a person doesn't conform when confronted with peer pressure, his behavior can be explained by means of a different causal law. Scientists have discovered so many causal laws that we are justified, I believe, in thinking that all of our behavior is governed by causal laws.

FREDERICK: Well, that seems to me to be nothing more than a mere hope, not based on good, solid evidence. Besides, you still have my second point to contend with, namely, that there is actual evidence against determinism.

DANIEL: What is that evidence?

FREDERICK: It's evidence that scientists have discovered in a branch of physics called quantum physics, or microphysics. In the early part of the twentieth century, physicists began studying the behavior of electrons, photons and other subatomic particles. What they found was that the movements of individual electrons and photons were random. There was nothing that explained why an electron or photon moved as it did. For example, it was discovered that electrons sometimes jump from one orbit to another without any apparent cause. And in the "shooting photon" experiment, it was found that when photons were shot at a barrier with two holes in it, it was impossible to explain why individual photons went through one hole rather than another.

DANIEL: Haven't scientists discovered any laws governing the behavior of subatomic particles?

FREDERICK: Yes, they have, but many of the laws they have discovered are only statistical ones, which don't explain the behavior of individual electrons and photons. They explain only what groups of electrons and photons do *as groups*. For instance, in the shooting photon experiment, physicists can tell how many of the photons will go through each hole, but they can't tell which ones will go through which hole. And in the jumping electron phenomenon, physicists know that a certain percentage of electrons will suddenly jump to a new orbit, but they can't tell which ones will do it or when they will do it.

DANIEL: What do you think is the significance of these new discoveries?

FREDERICK: I think that quantum physics has revolutionized our view of reality. Previously, scientists assumed that every occurrence was causally explainable, but now quantum physics has shown that this assumption is not true. Some kinds of occurrences are random and uncaused.

CAROLYN: How would you respond to this, Daniel?

DANIEL: My first reaction would be to wonder whether quantum physics really has shown that some kinds of occurrences are uncaused. There is so much evidence for determinism that I think we should be very skeptical when anyone claims to have found something that is uncaused.

FREDERICK: That's what the quantum physicists said at first, too. But their new discoveries were so startling that many of them changed their minds.

DANIEL: The only thing quantum physics has shown, so far as I can tell, is that we don't know the causes of certain kinds of occurrences. But this is far different from knowing that the occurrences don't have causes.

FREDERICK: No, quantum physics has shown that there is an actual lack of causality in the subatomic realm, not just that we don't know the causes. Consider the case of the shooting photons. When physicists shoot a stream of photons at a barrier, they find that the photons don't hit the barrier all at the same place. Some of the photons hit the barrier at places other than the spot at which the photons are shot, in the same way that some of the light from a flashlight hits a wall at places other than the exact place at which the flashlight is aimed. This phenomenon is called the photon dispersion effect. There is nothing about the way the photons are shot that explains their different directions of travel. Each photon is shot in exactly the same way. So the situation conforms to Carolyn's description of an uncaused happening—same initial conditions but different outcomes.

DANIEL: I don't see how anyone could know that the initial conditions are exactly the same. The most that anyone can say is that no one has found what accounts for the different outcomes. In the future, someone may well discover what causes the photons to disperse.

FREDERICK: According to quantum physicists, we will never find the cause. In fact, they say, we literally cannot find the cause, because the only instruments physicists can use to detect the movements of subatomic particles are so much larger than the particles themselves that the movement of the particles is changed whenever the physicists attempt to observe the particles. This situation is just like trying to find how fast a marble is moving by throwing a basketball at it. Obviously, the marble is going to change its speed when the basketball hits it.

DANIEL: If what you say is correct, then it is, indeed, impossible for us ever to find the cause of the photon dispersion effect. But that's not the same as saying that there is no cause. There still may be a cause even though no one can ever find it.

CAROLYN: I agree. There is no method of observing that an occurrence has *no* cause. Here is an example. Suppose the light in this room were to come on suddenly and then five seconds later go off. We don't see the cause of this mysterious phenomenon, but neither do we see that it has no cause. Something of which we have no conception might have caused it. So we can't say that it has no cause, but only that we don't know what it is.

DANIEL: Right. And the same is true at the subatomic level. There may be something of which we presently have no conception that is causing the photon dispersion effect.

CAROLYN: This means that there is no way to disprove determinism. If determinism were false, no one could ever know it.

DANIEL: I have another reaction to what you have been saying, Frederick.

FREDERICK: What is it?

DANIEL: I'm wondering what the new discoveries in quantum physics have to do with free will. In order for them to be relevant, wouldn't it have to be shown that our actions are the result of the uncaused behavior of electrons and photons in our brains?

FREDERICK: Yes, that's right.

DANIEL: Well, then, I don't see how the new discoveries are relevant, because scientists haven't shown that the uncaused activities of subatomic particles produce our free actions. But until they do show this, it is entirely possible that everything we do is determined, even if occurrences at the subatomic level are uncaused.

FREDERICK: It seems to me that if occurrences at the subatomic level are uncaused, then it is much more likely that some ordinary-level occurrences are uncaused.

DANIEL: No, that doesn't follow, because there is a huge amount of evidence for ordinary-level occurrences being caused. This means we can safely believe that all of our actions are caused, regardless of what quantum physics says about subatomic phenomena.

WHETHER DETERMINISM IS AN EMPIRICAL THEORY

CAROLYN: What is your reaction to Daniel's and my statement that we cannot observe that an occurrence has no cause, Frederick?

FREDERICK: If that statement is true, then you and Daniel cannot use observations to show that every occurrence has a cause, contrary to what you have been trying to do.

DANIEL: Why do you say that Carolyn and I can't do what we have been doing?

FREDERICK: Because if you say that we cannot observe that an occurrence has no cause, then you have to say that determinism is not an empirical theory. And if you say that determinism is not an empirical theory, then you can't say that science and everyday observations show it is true.

DANIEL: Could you explain that in more detail?

FREDERICK: Yes. In order for a statement to be empirical, it has to be refutable in principle. This means that we have to be able to think of some observable circumstance which, if it were to exist, would disprove the statement. If a statement is not refutable in principle—if, in other words, there isn't even any *possible* observation that would disprove it—it cannot be empirical. Would you say that's a fair description of an empirical statement?

DANIEL: Yes. That's the way it is normally described.

FREDERICK: Well, then, I don't see how you can say both that "Everything that happens has a cause" is an empirical statement *and* that there aren't any possible observations that would show that a happening doesn't have a cause. If there aren't any possible observations that would show that a happening doesn't have a cause, then determinism would not be refutable in principle, in which case it would not be empirical, according to the description to which you just agreed. That means that your appeal to empirical evidence in support of determinism would be quite beside the point. It wouldn't have the slightest relevance to whether or not determinism is true.

CAROLYN: It looks as if he has you in a trap, Daniel.

DANIEL: Aren't you in the same trap?

CAROLYN: No, because I didn't admit that empirical statements have to be both supportable *and* refutable in principle by empirical evidence. Some empirical statements, such as "Everything that happens has a cause," are supported by empirical evidence but are not refutable in principle by empirical evidence.

FREDERICK: The very definition of an empirical statement says that it has to be able to be refuted, in principle, by empirical evidence. If there isn't even any *possible* empirical evidence that would go against a statement, then the statement cannot be empirical. For instance, I know what would show the statement that all blades of grass are green to be false—a blade of grass that was orange or blue. We have to know what observable circumstance would make a statement false, even if it is true in actuality, in order to say that it is empirical.

CAROLYN: Here is an empirical statement that can be supported by empirical evidence but can't be refuted even in principle: "There is at least one thing in existence." It is an empirical statement because we can show it to be true by means of observations. But there isn't any possible observation we could use to show it to be false, because if it were false, nothing would exist, including ourselves. So the definition of an empirical statement is that *either* it has to be supportable in principle *or* it has to be refutable in principle.

FREDERICK: That violates the normal definition of "empirical." It has to be *both* supportable in principle and refutable in principle, even though it might actually be true, or actually false. Besides, my point is more than just a verbal one about the meaning of the word "empirical." If I can think of a possible circumstance that would show a statement to be true, then I should be able to think of a possible circumstance that would show that statement to be false. For instance, if I say there is a little red house on the other side of Jupiter, I know what would have to exist in order for it to be true. And I also know what circumstance would make it false. If I went there and looked everywhere but didn't see any little red house, it would be false. So if there aren't even any *possible* circumstances that would falsify a statement, then there aren't any possible circumstances that would verify a statement. That means that you are being inconsistent in trying to show that determinism is true on empirical grounds yet saying that there is nothing that could show that happenings don't have causes.

DANIEL: Well, there is something that would show that happenings don't have causes, namely, the circumstance of happenings not having causes. It's just that we could never know that that circumstance exists, if it does.

FREDERICK: That sounds like doubletalk. If there is some circumstance that would show determinism to be false if the circumstance existed, then it would be possible, theoretically at least, for us to know that determinism is false.

DANIEL: What I meant was that there is no way in which we, as limited, finite beings, can know that events don't have causes. For one thing, as Carolyn said, we don't ever observe events being uncaused. Also, if we look for the cause of an event and don't find it, we can't conclude that the event has no cause, because no matter how long we look, it is still possible that it has a cause and that we haven't looked long enough for it. We would know that events don't have causes only if we knew everything there is to know about the universe. We don't know everything, obviously, so we aren't able to know that events don't have causes.

FREDERICK: Are you saying that showing that an event doesn't have a cause is like showing that there are no dandelions in Brazil's jungles? Dandelions don't usually grow in jungles. But they could. So to show that they don't, we would have to look. And, of course, we could never go over every square foot of Brazil's jungles. Thus, we could never know for sure that there are no dandelions there.

DANIEL: Yes. The universe is so complicated that we could never be sure that we had looked at everything that we needed to in order to say that a certain event had no cause. If we found that a certain event, A, was not the cause of another event, E, there still might be another event, B, which was the cause of event E. And if we found that event B was not the cause of E, there still might be another event, C, which was the cause of event E. The possible causes of event E are so many that we could never be sure that we had exhausted them all.

FREDERICK: Tell me, Daniel, if you were looking for dandelions in the jungles of Brazil, and you spent several years carefully examining the ground for them, and did not find any, wouldn't you say that it is fairly probable that there weren't any, even though you had covered only one percent of all the jungles?

DANIEL: Yes, that sounds reasonable.

FREDERICK: If you say "Yes" in this dandelion case, then it seems to me you should say "Yes" to a similiar question about causes. Suppose you were looking for the cause of a certain type of event, and you spent several years carefully performing experiments in an effort to find it, but you did not find it. Wouldn't you say that it is fairly probable that such a cause doesn't exist, even though you had not performed all the possible experiments?

DANIEL: No, because there are many cases in which people have found the cause of a certain type of event only after looking for it a very long time. If I use your jungle metaphor, what it comes to is that people often before have looked in jungles for dandelions, and they haven't found them at first, but after much searching, they finally have found some. That being the case, if I were looking in some new jungle and didn't find any dandelions right away, I wouldn't conclude that probably there weren't any.

FREDERICK: I'm beginning to wonder whether you really think that "Every event has a cause" is an empirical statement. You don't seem to think that there is any possible circumstance which, if it existed, would show that events don't have causes. That makes it look as if you really believe determinism can be known to be true independently of experience.

DANIEL: I do think that "Every event has a cause" is an empirical statement, and I don't think that it can be known to be true independently of experience.

FREDERICK: I know you *say* that, but I'm wondering whether you can *consistently* say that in view of the fact that you also say that it isn't possible for us to obtain any evidence which would show that events don't have causes. If it is not possible for us to obtain any evidence which would show that events don't have causes, then it is not possible for us to obtain any evidence which would support determinism. That means that "Every event has a cause" is not an empirical statement, as you claim it is.

DANIEL: Well, it surely isn't like "Every father has a child" or "Every effect has a cause." Those statements aren't empirical because we can know that they are true just by knowing the meanings of the words in them. To be a father means to have a child, and to be an effect means being caused by something. If you look in the dictionary, you will find that "father" means "a man who has a child." And you will find that "effect" means "something produced by a cause." But you won't find that "event" means "occurrence that has a cause." It means just plain "occurrence" or "something that happens." So "Every event has a cause" is like "Every man is courageous in the face of great danger." We can't tell that these statements are true just by knowing the meanings of the words in them.

FREDERICK: I agree with you about all that. But that still doesn't show that "Every event has a cause" can be known to be true on the basis of experience. It might be a special statement which is neither empirical nor like "Every father has a child," and which you believe to be true because of a special insight you believe you have. If you say that there isn't any way to show that events don't have causes, then one wonders whether you *really* believe determinism to be true on the basis of empirical evidence. Maybe you believe it to be true because of an intuition that isn't based on any observations or experiences.

DANIEL: No, I really don't. There is empirical evidence for the truth of determinism, namely, many instances of events having causes. Determinism is like the statement "Every man is courageous." We have to observe whether or not men are courageous in order to find out whether or not the statement is true. If we didn't observe any men at all to see whether or not they are courageous, we wouldn't know what to believe about that statement. And if we didn't observe any events at all to see whether or not they have causes, we wouldn't know what to believe about determinism. We don't have any special nonempirical intuition that tells us that every event has a cause. At least I don't.

FREDERICK: If there is observational evidence that supports determinism, then not only should we be able to think of circumstances that show that events *do* have causes, but we should also be able to think of circumstances which, if they were to exist, would show that events *don't* have causes. But you said before that there is no amount of evidence which would show that events don't have causes. So I don't see how you can say that there is observational evidence that supports determinism.

DANIEL: What you want me to convince you of, I take it, is that I can conceive of a possible circumstance which, if it existed, would refute determinism. Is that right?

FREDERICK: Yes, that's right.

DANIEL: Well, if we never, or only rarely, found the causes of events, I would think that determinism is not very probable. In other words, not ever, or only rarely, finding causes of events would be empirical evidence against the probability of determinism.

FREDERICK: Didn't you say before that not finding the causes of events doesn't show that there aren't any?

DANIEL: Yes.

FREDERICK: Then you are being inconsistent. If not finding the causes of events doesn't show that the events don't have causes, then not finding the causes of events can't count as evidence against the probability of determinism, as you just said it could.

DANIEL: But the two cases are different.

FREDERICK: What two cases?

DANIEL: Never, or only rarely, finding the causes of events, on the one hand, and not finding the causes of events, on the other.

FREDERICK: Your distinction between "never" and "not" escapes me.

DANIEL: If we never found the causes of *any* events, or if we found the causes of only a few events, even though we looked hard and long, I would say that it was very probable that some events don't have causes. But since we have already found a huge amount of causes of events, it is probable that any given event does have a cause, even if we have not found it after looking hard and long. So as things stand, we cannot say that events don't have causes just because we have not found them, although we could say this if we had not already found so many causes.

FREDERICK: I'm still not satisfied that you have established that "Every event has a cause" is empirical. Your possible circumstance which, if it existed, would show determinism to be false consists only of not finding the causes of events, instead of finding that events do not have causes. But to show that "Every event has a cause" is empirical, you have to demonstrate that there is a possible circumstance in which we can determine that an event has no cause.

DANIEL: Never finding the causes of events would show that some events, at least, probably don't have causes.

FREDERICK: What circumstance, if it existed, would show that a *single* event has no cause? Unless you can answer that question, I don't see how you can maintain that "Every event has a cause" is empirical.

DANIEL: I don't think it is possible for us ever to know that a single event has no cause, because we don't ever observe an event having no cause. The most we could ever say is that a long and hard search for the cause of an event is a failure. And that's not sufficient for us to show that the event has no cause. However, if we knew everything there is to know about the universe, we would know of any event in the universe either that it has a cause or that it doesn't. So it is possible, in principle, though not for us as humans, to know that a single event has no cause.

CAROLYN: I would be interested in knowing how you would show that something doesn't have a cause, Frederick. What evidence do you think disproves determinism?

FREDERICK: There are two kinds of evidence that I think disprove determinism: twentieth-century advances in quantum physics, as I have already explained, and evidence that shows we have free will.

DELIBERATION AND FREE WILL

DANIEL: What evidence shows that we have free will?

FREDERICK: The fact that we deliberate, choose, think, confront alternatives and are directly aware of ourselves acting freely.

DANIEL: How do any of those things show that people have free will?

FREDERICK: Take deliberation. Suppose I am deliberating about whether or not to go to a concert. I have two alternatives. Either I can go to the concert or I can do something else, such as staying home and reading a book. That means I have a choice, because there is more than one thing I can do. If there were only one thing I could do, I would have no choice and I could not deliberate about what to do. But since I do deliberate about what to do, I have a choice, and, therefore, have free will.

DANIEL: Why can't our deliberations be caused by happenings over which we have no control?

FREDERICK: We can't deliberate about what we are going to do unless we can choose differently from the way we actually choose. And that means we can't deliberate about what we are going to do unless our deliberations are not caused by happenings over which we have no control.

DANIEL: I'm not convinced that that's so. Here's a case that shows we can deliberate about what we are going to do even though our deliberations are caused by happenings over which we have no control. Physiologists and neurosurgeons know enough about our brains and central nervous systems to be able to cause us to move parts of our bodies and have certain images and thoughts. They do these things by touching an electrically charged electrode to certain parts of the brain. Of course, they can't cause us to do everything, but a number of experiments have been done, and scientists are learning which parts of the brain control which activities. As of now, they don't know how to cause us to think and deliberate and choose, but it is possible that they will know how to do this at some time in the future. Suppose that time comes, and a physiologist touches an electrode to just the right part of my brain so as to cause me to deliberate about doing something. He then causes me to choose one of the alternatives that he has caused me to think about, and lastly, he touches the part of my brain that causes me to do what I have chosen to do. If these things were to happen, I would be deliberating and choosing among alternatives, even though my deliberations and choice were caused by happenings over which I have no control. That shows that it is possible for our deliberations to be caused by happenings over which we have no control. And that means you can't use the fact of deliberation to prove that we have free will.

FREDERICK: I don't think your case refutes my argument, because it is not a case in which you are really deliberating about what you are going to do. The physiologist would be manipulating what you think, choose and do, so you wouldn't be free. You would be just like a puppet, except that the strings attached to you would be electrically charged electrodes.

DANIEL: But the physiologist was causing me to do exactly what I do in daily life when I deliberate. How can you say that I was not deliberating?

FREDERICK: You weren't deliberating when the physiologist was touching electrodes to your brain because you weren't able to choose differently from the way you actually chose—there was only one thing you could choose, namely, the thing the physiologist caused you to choose.

DANIEL: When we deliberate in daily life, we weigh alternatives, think about consequences, evaluate reasons for doing things and make decisions. These are the very things I was doing when the physiologist was touching electrodes to my brain.

FREDERICK: You are right in saying that we weigh alternatives, think about consequences, evaluate reasons and make decisions when we deliberate. But that's not all that deliberation involves. It also involves the ability to choose differently from the way we actually choose. For instance, I could have chosen to stay home and read a book last night instead of going to a concert. Or I could have chosen to have an orange for breakfast instead of apple juice.

DANIEL: It is certainly true that when we deliberate in daily life we *think* we can choose differently from the way we actually choose. Otherwise, we wouldn't deliberate. But *thinking* we can choose differently doesn't show that we can *actually* choose differently. What makes you think it is the latter and not just the former that deliberation involves?

FREDERICK: A physiologist could cause us to *think* that we can choose differently. But if he did so, we wouldn't be deliberating. So deliberation must involve more than just thinking we can choose differently—we have to be able actually to choose differently.

DANIEL: If you are going to say that we can't deliberate unless we are actually able to choose differently, then it is far from obvious, at least to me, that we actually do deliberate. I don't want to say that we don't deliberate any more than you do. I think that we do deliberate—we weigh alternatives, consider consequences, evaluate reasons and make decisions. But doing these things doesn't presuppose that we can actually choose one thing rather than another, because they all can be caused by what goes on inside us—by brain states, for example, as my physiologist case shows, or by unconscious motives. So if you are going to use deliberation to refute determinism, you have to prove that we deliberate in a sense that clearly conflicts with determinism.

FREDERICK: We deliberate in a sense that clearly conflicts with determinism because the very concept of thinking about what we are going to do is linked to the concept of being able to choose differently from what we actually choose. When we think about doing something, we have the ability to choose to do it, and we also have the ability not to choose to do it. So no matter what we actually choose to do, we could have chosen differently. But if what we choose to do is determined, then we cannot choose differently, because there is only one thing we can choose, namely, that which we are determined to choose. So if we deliberate about what we are going to do, determinism has to be false.

DANIEL: I thought my physiologist case disproved that.

FREDERICK: You weren't really deliberating.

DANIEL: Take this case, then. Suppose you are hypnotized, and the hypnotist gives you a posthypnotic suggestion. He tells you that after you regain consciousness you will become thirsty. You will then deliberate about whether to get up and get a drink. You will think about whether it is worth the effort and about whether you would prefer water or orange juice. Finally, you will decide to get a drink of water. And then you will actually get up and do it. Now suppose that that is what you actually do. You go through the process of thinking, deciding and acting. Yet the entire process is caused by happenings that are beyond your control. You deliberate about what you are going to do even though you cannot choose or act differently from the way you actually choose and act. What would you say about this case?

FREDERICK: I would say that I wasn't really deliberating, because the hypnotist's posthypnotic suggestion was causing me to think and act as I did.

DANIEL: Well, it seems to me you're cheating, because every time I give you a case in which someone is deliberating but isn't free, you say he isn't really deliberating. I think that shows you are in a dilemma. If you admit that we are deliberating in the two cases I have described, then you also have to admit that deliberation does not disprove determinism. But if you say that we are not deliberating in those cases, then one wonders how you could show that we *ever* deliberate. What we think about in those cases is exactly what we think about in every other case in which anyone would say we deliberate. So either way, you can't prove that determinism is false.

FREDERICK: Your dilemma doesn't apply to me because there *are* times when we deliberate, thus disproving determinism.

DANIEL: To disprove determinism, you have to show that our deliberations cannot be caused by happenings over which we have no control. But I don't see how you could ever show that.

THE AWARENESS OF FREE WILL

FREDERICK: We can know that our deliberations are not caused by happenings over which we have no control because we directly apprehend ourselves being able to choose and act differently from the way we actually choose and act. And we can't have this direct apprehension unless our deliberations are not caused.

DANIEL: Could you give an example of that direct apprehension?

FREDERICK: Yes. Suppose I'm walking home from school and there are two ways I could go. Each way is the same length as the other, and neither is prettier, or more convenient, or less dangerous than the other. There is nothing about one of the ways that would make me decide for it rather than the other. In this circumstance, I am directly aware of myself being confronted with two possible courses of action. I am aware of myself being able to do either one, and when I choose one of them, I am aware of my choice being free and unhindered. After I choose one path, I have the awareness that I could have chosen the other.

DANIEL: How much weight do you attach to the awareness of being free?

FREDERICK: I think that the introspective evidence for free will is one of the strongest reasons for rejecting determinism. Our conviction that we can choose and act differently in different circumstances is based on immediate and self-evident intuitions of our ability to choose and act differently. Denying these immediate intuitions would seem to be a flagrant denial of the facts.

CAROLYN: Well, nobody wants to be in the position of flagrantly denying the facts. The real questions are whether or not what you say are facts really are facts, and whether or not those facts really show what you say they show.

DANIEL: Yes. It looks to me as if you're saying that we could have acted or decided differently because we have the feeling that we could have acted or decided differently. Such arguments are notoriously unreliable. I could argue that it will rain this afternoon because I have the feeling that it will rain.

FREDERICK: There is an obvious difference between the two cases. Your feeling that it will rain this afternoon isn't a direct observation of anything. It's more like a hunch. But our awareness that we can decide differently from the way we actually decide isn't a hunch. It's an immediate observation of our choices, like seeing and touching, except that the object is inside us. If you're going to be skeptical about our intuitions of free will, you should also be skeptical about seeing and touching.

DANIEL: Intuition is much more suspect than seeing and

touching. If you're wondering whether there is a tree over there, you can get a lot of people to look, and presumably everyone will see the same thing. But when you ask about people's intuitions, you will find nearly as many different intuitions as people.

FREDERICK: If the awareness of being able to choose and act differently were like that, I might have some doubts about using it as a proof for free will. But it isn't. Everyone has had the same awareness. Just try introspecting. The option of moving your arm is now open to you. You have the immediate intuition that it is up to you whether or not you do it. Now move it. Go ahead. Don't just imagine what it would be like. Actually experience it.

(Daniel moves his arm.)

FREDERICK: Okay. Now you have the immediate intuition that you could have refrained from doing it. Maybe there are people who have never stopped to think about what they experience in such circumstances. But if you point it out to them, they will immediately agree.

DANIEL: I guess you are right about everyone having the same intuition. However, intuitions are so unreliable in other cases that I don't see why we should trust them in this case.

FREDERICK: We should trust our intuitions of free choice because everyone has had exactly the same intuition. If one hundred people see a tree in my back yard, it would be absurd to say that there is no tree there. Similarly, it is unreasonable to doubt that we are able to choose and act differently from the way we actually choose and act, because everyone intuits himself having this ability.

DANIEL: I think my hesitancy to trust our intuitions of free will stems from the fact that it is possible for them to be mistaken. It is possible for us to intuit our choices and actions being free, even though they are not actually free. This means that our intuitions of free will don't show that we really have free will.

FREDERICK: By using similar reasoning, you could prove that seeing things doesn't show that they exist. It is possible for us to see things even though they don't exist. Mirages and hallucinations prove that. If it is possible for us to see things even though they don't exist, then, according to your reasoning, the fact that we see things doesn't prove that they exist. If that's so, then you can't be sure that anything we see exists. But that's absurd. So your argument is unsound, because it leads to an absurd result.

DANIEL: Let me give you an illustration of an unfree action that is intuited to be free. Suppose you were hypnotized and the hypnotist suggested to you that five minutes after you ceased being hypnotized you would debate with yourself about whether to read a certain book. You would decide to read the book and then you would actually start reading it. Now suppose that that is what you did. While you were debating to yourself, you were aware that you were able to decide in favor of reading the book, and you were aware that you were able to decide against reading the book. After you decided, you were aware that whether or not you read the book was up to you and that you were in control of whether or not you did it. After you began reading, you had the immediate intuition that you could have refrained from reading the book. But your choice and action were in reality caused by the suggestion of the hypnotist while you were hypnotized. So you weren't in control of what you did. It was determined, and you were the subject of forces beyond your control. This case shows that it is possible for us to have intuitions of free will even though our choices and actions are not free. And that means that our intuitions of free will don't prove that we actually have free will. What we are directly aware of as being free might actually be unfree.

FREDERICK: Suppose *you* were hypnotized and the hypnotist suggested to you that five minutes after you regained consciousness you would see a baby giraffe walking around the room. You wake up and five minutes later you see a baby giraffe walking around the room. It's not really there, of course, but you see it, because the hypnotist made you see it. Better yet, suppose that there is a cosmic hypnotist who has hypnotized everybody and has caused everyone to see the very things we now see. Nothing would exist besides ourselves, but we would still be seeing things. These cases are possible. And if your reasoning about free will and the awareness of free will is sound, then these possibilities show that seeing things isn't sufficient evidence for our knowing that they actually exist.

DANIEL: Are you saying that our intuitions of free will are like our perceptions of physical things?

FREDERICK: Yes. If the possibility of our intuitions of free will being mistaken shows that they do not prove that we have the ability to act differently from the way we actually act, then the possibility of our external perceptions being mistaken shows that they do not prove that physical objects exist. But if external perceptions such as seeing and touching show that physical objects really exist, then our intuitions of being able to act differently show that we really are able to act differently from the way we actually act.

DANIEL: Intuitions are different from our perception of physical things. We can corroborate seeing a tree by touching it. But there is no way we can corroborate an intuition of free will.

FREDERICK: Yes there is. I can corroborate an intuition of free will by having the same intuition on many different occasions and by asking other people whether or not they have the same intuition.

DANIEL: But everyone could be mistaken.

FREDERICK: Everyone could be mistaken in thinking that he sees and touches a tree.

CAROLYN: If your parallel between intuitions and external perceptions is correct, Frederick, then our intuitions of free will show that we actually have free will.

FREDERICK: Yes, that's right.

CAROLYN: Of course, someone could say that neither our intuitions of free will nor our external perceptions establish the existence of anything.

FREDERICK: Surely, no one would go so far as to say that. You wouldn't say that, would you, Daniel?

DANIEL: No. What I say is that your parallel between intuitions of free will and external perceptions is not correct. But even if your parallel is correct, I don't have to say that our intuitions of free will show that we actually have free will. I can say that all of our intuitions of free will are mistaken. That, in fact, is what I do say. The amount of scientific evidence for there being causal explanations of all our choices and actions is so overwhelming that we cannot avoid concluding that our intuitions of free will are mistaken.

FREDERICK: When we compare the evidence for free will with the evidence against it, what we find is that our intuitions of free will are stronger evidence for free will than your appeal to science is against free will.

DANIEL: Why do you say that?

FREDERICK: In the first place, everyone has had immediate intuitions of being able to act differently from the way he actually acts. In the second place, the intuitions are strong. They are evident and obvious. We aren't mistaken about what they are. It's like feeling warm. We know when we feel warm, and that's all there is to it. Both of these points mean that we have actual evidence for free will. But we don't have actual causal explanations for all of the things we do. You admit that. And scientists admit it, too. There wouldn't be any need for further research if scientists had already discovered everything there is to know. Now put the first two points next to this last point. In the one case, we have actual evidence. In the other case, we have only hoped-for evidence. If we're rational and objective about the matter, we should choose the side that has the actual evidence.

DANIEL: There *is* actual evidence for determinism, not just hoped-for evidence. The amount of scientific evidence we now have makes it very likely that all of our choices and actions have causal explanations, even though we don't know now what all of the explanations are. The actual evidence for that likelihood is stronger evidence for determinism than your appeal to intuition is against determinism. Don't you agree, Carolyn?

Whether the Awareness of Free Will Conflicts with Determinism

CAROLYN: I'm not sure how to answer that question. On the one hand, the evidence for determinism is so strong that it would be unreasonable to disbelieve it. Yet, as Frederick says, the awareness of free will is so clear and pervasive that it would be unreasonable to deny that people have free will. Fortunately for me, I don't have to choose between the evidence for determinism and our intuitions of free will, as you do, because I don't think that our intuitions of free will conflict with determinism.

FREDERICK: How does that differ from what Daniel says?

CAROLYN: Daniel thinks that if our intuitions of being able to act differently were correct, determinism would be false. In other words, he thinks that our intuitions of being able to act differently conflict with determinism. Since he also thinks that the evidence for determinism outweighs the evidence for free will, he says that our intuitions of free will are mistaken. We intuit ourselves being free, but we aren't really. Is that right, Daniel?

DANIEL: Right.

CAROLYN: I say, however, that determinism can be true even though our intuitions of being able to act differently are correct. In other words, our intuitions of being able to act differently don't conflict with determinism. So I don't have to say that our intuitions are mistaken, as Daniel does, in order to maintain determinism. I can say that they show that we have free will. Of course, if our intuitions of being able to act differently don't conflict with determinism, then they don't disprove determinism.

FREDERICK: I'd like to see you make a case for our intuitions not conflicting with determinism, because it certainly appears as if they do conflict. Determinism says that nothing we do could have been different. But we intuitively apprehend that we are able to act differently from the way we actually act.

CAROLYN: When we intuit that, we are not intuiting that we can act differently *even if* everything just prior to our actions were to remain the same. But unless we do intuit this, we are not intuiting anything that conflicts with determinism.

FREDERICK: Why do you say that?

CAROLYN: Suppose you were watching a walking robot. It walks up to a wall and then stops. At that point, it can go left, or it can go right, or it can turn around and walk away from the wall. Nothing in its immediate environment prevents the robot from doing any of these things. If it does happen to go to the left, it could have gone to the right instead. So it can act differently from the way it actually acts. But notice that it can act differently only with respect to its immediate *external* environment. It might have been programmed always to turn around and walk away from a wall it bumped into. If so, it could not act differently even if *everything* just prior to its action, including what goes on inside it, had remained the same. So if we intuit only that we can act differently with respect to our immediate external environment, we are not intuiting anything that goes against determinism. It might be that something *inside* us causes us to act as we do. What we need to intuit is that we can act differently even if everything, including what goes on inside us, were to remain the same.

FREDERICK: We do intuit that. Take moving an arm as an example. Before I move my arm, I am aware that I can move it in different directions. I can move it up, down, left, right, or not at all. It is the same with almost anything we do. And there is an easy way to test my claim—just introspect whenever you do or decide something.

CAROLYN: I have introspected. But I don't find that I can act differently even if everything inside me were to remain the same. The reason I don't find this is that I am not aware of everything that goes on inside me. I am not aware of anything that goes on in my brain, central nervous system or subconscious mind. So when I am aware that I can do any one of several different things, I am aware that there isn't anything *outside* me that prohibits me from doing them.

FREDERICK: I agree with you that with respect to external circumstances, we observe ourselves able to do a number of different things. But that's not all we intuit. Take the case of choosing between two ways to go home. Each way is of equal length, and each way is equal in every other respect. When we intuit our motives, we find that they are equal; that is, we do not intuit ourselves having a stronger motive to go one of the ways. And we intuit ourselves choosing freely between the two alternatives. There is nothing external or internal which we intuit to hinder us from choosing either alternative.

CAROLYN: We may intuit all of our conscious motives, but we certainly do not intuit any of our unconscious motives. Nor do we intuit anything in our brains. That means that when we intuit ourselves freely choosing one of several alternatives, we are intuiting that there are no *external* circumstances preventing us from doing what we want to do. That intuition is what constitutes the intuition of freedom. Notice, however, that the intuition doesn't have the slightest tendency to disprove determinism. There might be something *inside* us, such as an unconscious motive or part of our brain, that causes us to choose one alternative rather than another.

DANIEL: It occurs to me, Carolyn, that we don't have to intuit *everything* that goes on inside us in order to have an intuition that conflicts with determinism. We know that some things inside us won't cause us to move our arms or to choose one way to go home instead of another. Our stomachs, for instance, or the blood vessels in our fingers, don't influence us when deciding which way to go home. So we don't have to be aware of them in order to intuit something that conflicts with determinism.

CAROLYN: That's a good point. If we know that something inside us won't cause us to do something, then our intuitions of being able to act differently don't have to include that in order to conflict with determinism. But there are several things inside us that could cause us to do something. Brain states, for example. And unconscious motives. We aren't aware of any of these. But we would have to be aware of them in order for us to say that our intuitions of being able to act differently conflict with determinism.

DANIEL: I take it you think that applies to all of the different ways we are aware of our free will. Is that correct?

CAROLYN: Yes. No matter how our awarenesses of freedom are described, we still would have to be aware of our choices and actions being uncaused in order for our awarenesses to refute determinism.

FREDERICK: What about the awareness of being in control of what we do? Or the awareness of being able to choose freely among conflicting desires and impulses? Or the awareness of being able to perform either of two different movements of our body? Or the awareness that what we do, think and decide is up to us? Surely these disprove determinism!

CAROLYN: No, I don't think that any of them disproves determinism. When we have these intuitions, we are not intuiting that our actions, thoughts and decisions are uncaused, because we are not intuiting that we can act, think and decide differently even if everything inside us were to remain the same. But unless we do intuit that our actions, thoughts and decisions are uncaused, we are not intuiting anything that conflicts with determinism.

FREDERICK: Do you think our awarenesses of free will are mistaken?

CAROLYN: No. I think our awarenesses of free will are correct. They show that we have freedom, but they do not show that determinism is false.

WHETHER DETERMINISM IS COMPATIBLE WITH FREE WILL

FREDERICK: Perhaps we should turn to the question of whether determinism is compatible with free will.

CAROLYN: Okay.

DANIEL: That's okay with me, too, except that I don't see the need for much of a discussion since it seems obvious that no one can be both free and determined. If everything we do is determined, as you and I have been arguing, Carolyn, then nothing we do can be free.

FREDERICK: I agree. And if some of what we do is free, as I have been arguing, then not everything we do can be determined.

DANIEL: That seems so obvious that I wonder why anyone would seriously wonder otherwise.

CAROLYN: There is a good motive for seriously wondering otherwise. The evidence for determinism is so strong that one cannot help believing it. And the belief in free will is so evident that one cannot help believing it, either. That means that a person who thinks that free will and determinism are incompatible is in a predicament. He can't believe both, because they are incompatible, yet he has to believe both because of the evidence for them.

FREDERICK: One way for him to get out of that predicament is to deny determinism.

CAROLYN: I know. That's your way out. But I don't think it is a good way, because of the large amount of evidence for determinism.

DANIEL: Another way out of that predicament is to deny that people have free will.

CAROLYN: I know. That's your way. But the intuitive conviction of free will is so strong and widespread that I am reluctant to deny that people have free will. So the only thing left for me to do is to wonder seriously whether free will and determinism really do conflict.

FREDERICK: That's not a good reason for saying that they don't conflict, is it?

CAROLYN: No, not at all. It's just a motive for investigating the possibility of their not conflicting. As it turns out, there is a good reason for thinking that they don't conflict.

FREDERICK: What is it?

CAROLYN: To say that we are free is to say that there are no persons or external circumstances preventing us from doing what we want to do. And saying that we are free in this sense is compatible with saying that determinism is true.

FREDERICK: Why do you define freedom in that way?

CAROLYN: I define freedom in that way because those situations in which we say a person is free are situations in which no other person or circumstance prevents him from doing what he wants to do. And those situations in which we say a person is not free are situations in which there is some person or circumstance preventing him from doing what he wants to do or forcing him to do something he does not want to do. Let me illustrate. Suppose three people suddenly grab my arm and prevent me from moving it. I would not be free to scratch my nose because they would be preventing me from doing so. But as soon as they let go, I would be free again because they would not be preventing me from acting as I wish. Or suppose the government suddenly disenfranchised all suspected subversives. They would not be free to vote because the government would be preventing them from doing so. As it is now, they are free to vote because the government is not preventing them from doing so.

FREDERICK: Do you think people have freedom in your sense of the word "free"?

CAROLYN: Yes. There are lots of things we are not prevented from doing, and there are lots of things we are not forced to do. We can travel where we want to, vote in any way we wish, buy any house or car we want to, and so on. Of course, we are not free to do *anything* we want to, and sometimes we are forced to do things we do not want to do. In fact, throughout our lives we are hedged by people, circumstances and laws that constrict our freedom in various ways. So our freedom certainly is not absolute but it is, nevertheless, something we do have.

FREDERICK: Isn't it possible to take away all of a person's freedom by not permitting him to do anything?

CAROLYN: Yes, it certainly is possible, but it is hardly ever done. And even if a person were prevented from *doing* anything he wanted to do, he still could *think* whatever he wished. That is one freedom that is very difficult to take away.

FREDERICK: Do you think that everyone has the same amount of freedom in your sense of the word "free"?

CAROLYN: No. Some people have less freedom than others. People living under military dictatorships have less freedom than do people in other countries. Black people in the United States sometimes cannot obtain the job of their choice because white prejudice prevents them from doing so. But although some people are not as free as others, everyone has some measure of freedom, because no one is forced to do everything he does, and no one is prevented from doing everything he wants to do.

FREDERICK: I understand now what your conception of being free is. Could you explain why in your sense a person can be both free and determined?

CAROLYN: Yes. A person can be free *and* determined because what he does can be caused by something that goes on inside him even though he is not forced by some circumstance outside him to act as he does. If he is not forced by some circumstance outside him to act as he does, then he acts freely. Yet his action nonetheless could be caused by something inside him, such as an unconscious motive or a brain state.

FREDERICK: Am I right in saying that your position involves two separate statements—the first being a statement of what it means to be free, and the second being the statement that this conception of being free does not conflict with determinism?

CAROLYN: Yes.

FREDERICK: Your second statement is certainly true. *If* being free is the same as not being prevented by external circumstances from acting as we want to, then our actions could be caused even though they are done freely. Determinism could then be true even though some of our actions are done freely.

CAROLYN: What do you think about my first statement?

FREDERICK: I think it is false, because being free in your sense is not a genuine freedom. It is a bogus freedom, not worthy of the name at all.

CAROLYN: Why do you say that?

UNCONSCIOUS

FREDERICK: Because a person could have freedom in your sense even though he had no control over anything he does. Let me explain. If everything a person does were caused by unconscious motives, as you say, then he would have no control over anything he does. Unknown to him, he would be buffeted about by the workings of his unconscious mind. Yet such a person would have freedom in your sense of freedom because no external circumstances would prevent him from doing what he consciously wants to do. That means your conception of freedom is a sham—a person who has freedom in your sense does not have control over what he does.

CAROLYN: That is an interesting response to my position, but I don't think it discredits my concept of freedom. Whether or not something inside us causes us to act as we do is irrelevant to whether or not we are free. What counts is whether or not something outside us prevents us from acting as we wish. If nothing does, we are free.

FREDERICK: You can call that freedom if you want to, but it is a pseudofreedom. Suppose a very smart neurosurgeon could put a device into a person's brain that would cause him to do everything he does. He would be just like a robot. In no significant sense could he be said to have free will, because he would not have control over anything he does. He would not even have control over what he *wants* to do, because the device would cause him to want to do what he does. Yet he would have freedom in your sense of freedom, because no external barriers or obstacles prevent him from doing what he wants to do. So your conception of freedom is bogus—a "robot-person" who has freedom in your sense does not have any control over what he does. Who would want a freedom from external constraints if something else external to our conscious minds but inside our bodies, were controlling everything we do and think? That's no freedom at all!

CAROLYN: People everywhere want freedom from external constraints. And when it is lost, wars are sometimes fought to regain it.

FREDERICK: That's beside the point. You accept the findings of contemporary psychoanalysis, so you have to say that everything we do, think, choose and desire is caused by our unconscious minds. Our unconscious minds are just like the device put into the person's brain by the neurosurgeon. How, then, can anyone have genuine freedom?

CAROLYN: I base my concept of freedom on the way we ordinarily use the word "free." We say people are free to buy things at one store instead of another because nothing prevents them from doing so. We say people in China are not free to set up private businesses because they are prevented from doing so by the government.

FREDERICK: You are right in saying that we use "free" in those ways. But if that is the entire foundation for our concept of freedom, then freedom is nothing more than an absence of external constraints, which is not enough to constitute genuine human freedom.

CAROLYN: What more could be wanted in human freedom than an absence of external constraints?

UNCAUSED

FREDERICK: Uncaused choices and actions. If our freedom is simply an absence of external constraints, then it lacks the most important feature of free will—the ability to control what we do. To have this feature, our actions and choices must be uncaused.

CAROLYN: Why must our actions and choices be uncaused if they are to be in our control?

FREDERICK: In order for our actions and choices to be in our control, they must be able to be different even if everything prior to them were to remain the same. But that is just what it means to be uncaused. So in order for our actions and choices to be in our control, they must be uncaused.

CAROLYN: Could you explain all that in more detail?

FREDERICK: Yes. Let me begin with what it means to be uncaused. When you and Daniel were explaining why you believe in determinism, you said that something is uncaused if it is possible for it to be different even if everything occurring just prior to it were to remain the same. You gave an example of a tree being blown over by a strong wind. If a strong gust of wind did not blow a tree over on one occasion but did on another, then we would naturally think that the conditions immediately prior to the wind's hitting the tree were different each time. That's because we naturally think the wind *caused* the tree to fall over the second time. So when we think of something's being caused we think of it as not being able to be different unless something occurring just before it were also different. And, conversely, when we think of something's being *uncaused*, we think of it as being able to be different even though everything occurring just before it were the same. Does that sound right?

CAROLYN: Yes.

FREDERICK: Now let me relate this to the concept of being in control of what we do. We cannot be in control of what we do unless we are able to do something different from what we actually do. We have to be faced with genuine possibilities—there cannot be just one thing we can do. This applies both to our external environment and our internal states. In other words, in order to be in control of what we do, what we do has to be able to be different even though everything—both external and internal—just prior to what we do were to remain the same. Since that is what it means to be uncaused, what we do has to be uncaused if we are to be in control of it. So you cannot say that people are free *and* that determinism is true.

DANIEL: I like that argument.

FREDERICK: Thank you.

DANIEL: What do you think of it, Carolyn?

CAROLYN: It certainly is well thought out.

FREDERICK: Don't you agree with it?

CAROLYN: No. I don't think that actions must be uncaused in order to be free. In fact, I think just the opposite—in order to be free, actions *cannot* be uncaused. They must be *caused*.

FREDERICK: Why is that?

CHANCE

CAROLYN: Because being uncaused is the same as happening

as a result of pure chance. But, surely, we cannot be in control of what we do if it is pure chance whether or not we do it. A dice-throw conception of human freedom is certainly wrong.

FREDERICK: Why do you say that being uncaused is the same as happening as a result of pure chance?

CAROLYN: To be uncaused, as you just pointed out, involves being able to be different. And being able to be different is the same as pure chance—either one thing can happen or something else can happen. This means that free actions cannot be uncaused—any action that is a result of pure chance is not free.

DANIEL: How would you reply to that, Frederick?

FREDERICK: I would say that Carolyn is wrong in thinking that being uncaused is the same as pure chance. To be uncaused is the same as being able to act differently, to be sure, but being able to act differently is the essence of free will, not chance.

CAROLYN: Why is that so?

FREDERICK: Because being able to act differently is the same as being confronted with alternatives. And this, surely, is what free will is. How could it possibly be chance?

CAROLYN: It's chance because either alternative might happen. The case of the swerving electron illustrates this perfectly. When Daniel and I were arguing that determinism is true, you said that contemporary quantum physics has shown that electron movements are sometimes uncaused. For example, electrons sometimes jump from one orbit to another without any apparent cause. Some physicists interpret this phenomenon as a chance event. They do so because they think that the electron's swerve might have been different. But this is exactly what you say about free actions. So it seems to me that your concept of free action is no different from the concept of an electron's chance swerve.

FREDERICK: But there are clear and evident differences between the two cases.

CAROLYN: What are they?

FREDERICK: In the first place, a free action is something that a person produces, whereas an electron's uncaused swerve is something that happens to the electron. In the second place, a person's free action is usually done for a particular purpose, whereas obviously, an electron's swerve is not done for a purpose. These differences mean that a person's free actions are controlled by the person and are not a result of chance.

CAROLYN: You aren't saying that free actions are *caused* by persons or purposes, are you?

FREDERICK: No, not at all. A person does not cause his actions in the way that one happening causes another. He does, indeed, bring about his own actions, but this is different from one happening causing another, because a person is not a happening—he is an enduring individual. Nor does a purpose cause someone to act as he does. A purpose does, indeed, provide a reason for a person's acting as he does; but, again, this is different from one happening causing another, because purposes are not happenings. For example, a law student's goal to become a defense attorney explains why he is in law school, but it doesn't cause him to be there.

CAROLYN: That's a good example, but even so, I still think that your concept of free will involves chance just as much as the concept of an electron swerve does.

FREDERICK: Don't you think there are any differences between the two cases?

CAROLYN: Essentially, no. Since you deny determinism, you have to say that what a person does to bring about his actions is itself uncaused. And saying this brings you right back to the electron swerve. A person can either bring about his actions or not. This is just like saying that an electron can either swerve or not. And appealing to purposes doesn't remove the chance, because a person still can act in more than one way.

FREDERICK: Don't we normally distinguish between chance and nonchance on the basis of the absence or presence of a purpose? Don't we say, for instance, that two people met by chance if neither one intended to meet the other? And doesn't the presence of one person's intention to meet the other eliminate the element of chance from their meeting?

CAROLYN: No, I don't think it does if what they did was uncaused. An uncaused action is one that either might happen or might not. And this is what chance is. It makes no difference that the action is done for a purpose. So, again, a free action cannot be uncaused.

FREDERICK: If you say that actions must be caused in order to be free, don't you have to say that the causes also have to be caused in order for the actions to be free?

CAROLYN: Yes, that's right. What I have been saying about actions applies also to their causes.

FREDERICK: In that case, you have to say that in order to be free, our actions must have endless chains of causes, don't you?

CAROLYN: Yes. If we are to be in control of what we do, our actions must be caused, and the causes must be caused, and so on, forever.

FREDERICK: Well, I don't see how that can possibly be true. If we are in control of what we do, there has to be some point at which the chain of causes is broken—a point at which something is uncaused.

CAROLYN: Why do you say that?

BEFORE-BIRTH ARGUMENT

FREDERICK: Because if everything we do were caused, and if the causes of what we do were caused, and so on, there would be a chain of causes stretching back to happenings that occurred prior to our births. But we certainly do not have control over anything that happened prior to our births. You will admit that, I presume?

CAROLYN: Yes.

FREDERICK: Well, then, it follows that if everything we do were caused, we would have no control over anything we do, because everything we do would be caused ultimately by happenings over which we have no control. So there cannot be an endless chain of causes causing everything we do if our actions are free. Our actions, or the choices that cause our actions, must be uncaused if we are to be in control of what we do. That means that if people have free will, as I say, then determinism is false; and if determinism is true, as you and Daniel say, then people have no free will.

DANIEL: I agree with you. That is an excellent argument for the incompatibility of free will and determinism.

CAROLYN: Your argument sounds a little bit like Clarence Darrow's statement that "any one of an infinite number of causes reaching back to the beginning" made Leopold and Loeb commit murder.

FREDERICK: That's right. Of course, I disagree with Darrow's belief in determinism, but I agree with him that if everything we do is caused by events occurring before our births, then we have no free will.

DANIEL: What are your reactions to this argument, Carolyn?

CAROLYN: I think that we all have freedom even though everything we do is caused by happenings occurring prior to our births. That's because the way we decide in daily life whether or not we have freedom is to determine whether or not there is anything preventing us from doing what we want to do. If there isn't anything, then we have freedom, even though what we do is caused by an endless chain of happenings.

FREDERICK: Your response seems to me to sidestep the issue entirely. If everything we do is caused by happenings that occur prior to our births and over which we have no control, then we have no control over anything we do now, and, thus, we have no free will. Your claim about how we ordinarily decide whether or not someone has freedom, even if true, is quite irrelevant to this argument.

CAROLYN: The way in which we ordinarily decide whether or not someone has freedom is at the very heart of the issue. We have to have a conception of freedom before we can answer the question, "Are we free?" Our normal conception of what it means to be free is expressed by the phrase, "not being prevented from doing what we want to do." So the question becomes, "Are there times when we are not prevented from doing what we want to do?" and its answer is obvious—there are, lots of them. What happens before we are born has nothing to do with answering this question.

FREDERICK: That's true. But the question itself is wrong. The "freedom" it refers to is not at all what people have in mind when they talk about *free will.* What Daniel and I want to know, and what people down through the ages have wanted to know, is whether or not people have free will. What happens before we are born is most relevant to *this* question, because we cannot have any free will if our lives are products solely of what happens before our births, which would be the case if determinism were true.

CAROLYN: No, the question is not wrong, because the concept of freedom it contains is linked to other concepts which we all use in our daily lives. Both moral and legal accountability depend on the kind of freedom I have been defending, since a person cannot be held accountable for what he does if he is forced to do it. The legitimacy of punishment depends on freedom as I conceive it. And the very existence of moral obligations depends on the freedom I say we have, for it is absurd to suppose we have obligations if we have no freedom to fulfill them. So my concept of freedom cannot be eliminated from our thinking without wrenching a whole group of concepts from our daily thought patterns. That means that the way I understand the question "Are we free?" is right.

FREDERICK: I don't think it means that at all. Just because the concept of freedom is linked to those other concepts doesn't mean that your compatibilist concept of freedom is right. After all, *all* of those concepts—freedom, moral and legal accountability, punishment, and moral obligation—could conflict with determinism even though they are linked together. Besides, nothing you have said indicates what part of my before-birth argument you think is wrong.

CAROLYN: The part that is wrong is the part that says we have no freedom if everything we do is caused by happenings occurring prior to our births. This part is wrong because of the things I have been saying about our ordinary conception of freedom and its connection to other commonly used concepts.

FREDERICK: But surely we cannot have control over what we do if our lives are products solely of what happens before we are born. What could be more obvious?

CAROLYN: What could be more obvious than that a person is free when nothing prevents him from doing what he wants to do?

DANIEL: Maybe it is time we turned to another topic. You two are never going to convince each other.

SUMMARY

FREDERICK: Why don't we summarize our positions before we move on?

DANIEL: That's a good idea. I'll start. I think your criticisms of Carolyn's conception of freedom are good, Frederick. *If* we have free will, then what we do, think and choose has to be uncaused.

FREDERICK: You and I agree on that.

DANIEL: Yes, that's right. We disagree on whether we have free will and on whether determinism is true. I think that science and experience show that determinism is true—everything we do, think and choose is caused. I infer that we have no free will.

FREDERICK: I think that we do have free will, for the reasons I explained earlier—we deliberate about things we are going to do, and we are directly aware of ourselves acting and deciding freely. I infer that determinism is false—some things we do, think and choose are uncaused.

CAROLYN: I agree with Daniel that determinism is true. But I do not infer that people have no free will, as Daniel does, because I do not think that determinism and free will conflict.

FREDERICK: You and I agree, Carolyn, in rejecting Daniel's claim that people have no free will.

CAROLYN: Yes. Daniel believes in both determinism and the incompatibility of determinism and free will. Because of this he has to say that people have no choice at all about anything they do. I find that impossible to believe.

FREDERICK: So do I.

CAROLYN: But I find your position just as impossible to believe, Frederick, because it involves the absurd conception of a free action that is nothing more than pure chance. The obvious solution, it seems to me, is to say that freedom and determinism do not conflict.

FREDERICK: I think that involves a bogus conception of freedom, as I pointed out earlier. Besides, no one has yet succeeded in destroying my before-birth argument for the incompatibility of free will and determinism.

DETERMINISM AND MORAL RESPONSIBILITY

DANIEL: Shall we consider the question of moral responsibility now?

FREDERICK: Yes, let's do that. I'll begin by describing the problem that the determinist faces. What he must do is explain how people can be morally responsible for what they do, even though everything they do is caused.

DANIEL: Can you explain why you think that is a problem for the determinist?

FREDERICK: Yes. If everything we do were caused, as you say, then nothing we do could be different. And if nothing we do could be different, we would not be morally responsible for anything we do. To be morally responsible for something, there has to be more than one thing we can do. It can't be that we *have* to do something. Do you agree to these things?

DANIEL: Yes.

FREDERICK: Then it follows that we are not morally responsible for anything we do if everything we do is caused.

DANIEL: Yes, I agree. Determinism and moral responsibility are incompatible. A person can't consistently believe both. But that's not a problem for the determinist unless there are decisive reasons for thinking that we actually are morally responsible for what we do. After all, the determinist can simply deny that we are ever morally responsible.

FREDERICK: No, he can't do that, because there are decisive reasons for believing in moral responsibility.

DANIEL: My response to that is to say that the evidence for determinism is so strong that we should believe it even if that means denying moral responsibility. What you think are good reasons for believing in moral responsibility really aren't, because the evidence for determinism shows that we aren't morally responsible for anything we do.

FREDERICK: That certainly is an extreme position to take. It goes against what nearly everyone believes about human nature, and it goes against plain and evident facts that show we are morally responsible beings.

DANIEL: To what facts are you referring?

FREDERICK: I'm referring to praise, blame, reward, punishment, guilt, remorse, the criminal justice system, and morality. All of these presuppose that we are morally responsible for what we do.

DANIEL: No, they don't presuppose that. They make sense even though everything we do is caused by happenings over which we have no control and even though we are not morally responsible for anything we do.

FREDERICK: I don't see how that can be true. It makes no sense to blame or punish someone for something he does unless he is morally responsible for it. And it makes no sense to judge the rightness or wrongness of something a person does unless he has control over it. How can you deny these obvious truths?

DANIEL: I don't think they are obvious truths. In fact, I think they are wrong, because the whole point of blaming and punishing people is to deter them from hurting other people and to protect other people from being hurt. Furthermore, morality is nothing more than a system of likes and dislikes. Since deterring, protecting, liking and disliking are all compatible with determinism and the denial of moral responsibility, it follows that blame, punishment and morality are all compatible with determinism and the denial of moral responsibility.

FREDERICK: Can you explain that in more detail?

BLAME AND PUNISHMENT

DANIEL: Yes. I'll start with the first point. When we blame someone for doing something wrong or punish him for breaking the law, we do so because we want to prevent him from doing it again and because we want to prevent other people from doing it at all. When we praise someone for doing something good or reward him for doing something beneficial to society, we do so because we want to encourage him and others to do it again. These motives are the reason we prosecute people who break the law, and they are the reason we discipline our children and praise them for their achievements.

FREDERICK: How is that supposed to refute my claim that blame and punishment make sense only if people are morally responsible for what they do?

DANIEL: Encouraging people to act in certain ways, trying to change their behavior patterns, and preventing them from hurting others do not presuppose that people are morally responsible for what they do. These activities presuppose only that there is a strong probability that the person to whom they are directed will be caused to act differently. That's why it is not pointless to blame a person for his misdeeds, and why it is pointless to blame a rock for breaking a window, even though neither the person nor the rock is morally responsible for anything he or it does. All of this means that blaming, praising and punishing make sense even though everything we do is caused by happenings over which we have no control and even though we are not morally responsible beings.

FREDERICK: It sounds to me as if you would disagree with

Clarence Darrow's strategy of using determinism to try to save his clients from being hanged.

DANIEL: Yes, that's right. Although I agree with Darrow's belief in determinism, I don't think determinism can be used as an excuse to avoid blame and punishment.

FREDERICK: I certainly agree with you that we use blame and punishment to get people to change their behavior and to protect other people from harm. But if that is all there is to blaming and punishing, then I think you have missed a crucial requirement for their legitimate use.

DANIEL: What requirement are you referring to?

FREDERICK: The avoidance requirement, which says that a person should be blamed or punished for doing something only if he could have avoided doing it. Suppose, for instance, that a person is forced at gun-point to drive the get-away car in a bank robbery, or suppose that a person accidentally trips and knocks down a bystander whose arm is broken as a result of the encounter. In neither case could the person have avoided what he did. So in neither case would it be legitimate to blame him and to say he has done something morally wrong. Nor would it be legitimate to prosecute the first person for complicity in a bank robbery, and the second for assault and battery. This avoidance requirement is so widely accepted that any conception of blaming and punishing that denies it should be seriously questioned. And, also, you will notice that the avoidance requirement makes blame and punishment incompatible with determinism. If determinism were true, then nothing we do could be different; everything we do would have to be done and could not be avoided. So if determinism were true, blaming and punishing should be abandoned because they would violate the avoidance requirement.

DANIEL: I agree with you that determinism entails that nothing we do can be avoided. But that doesn't mean blame and punishment should be abandoned, because the avoidance principle is not a requirement for their legitimate use. The only requirements are that the behavior in question be undesirable, and that the blaming or punishing help prevent that kind of behavior. These requirements are not met in your two examples, because in neither case would blame and punishment help prevent people from doing those things. For instance, we don't punish someone who accidentally trips and knocks down a bystander, because blaming and punishing would not deter him or other people from tripping again. By contrast, blaming and punishing would deter people from deliberately knocking down other people.

FREDERICK: How can blame and punishment deter people from doing something unless people are able to avoid doing it?

DANIEL: Blame and punishment deter people from doing certain things because they cause people's *later* actions to be different from their former actions. Blame and punishment do not presuppose that the *very* action for which a person is blamed could have been avoided.

FREDERICK: If punishment is permissible even though people are not able to avoid what they do, then how can there be a distinction between punishing someone for something he has done and treating him for an illness he has? Isn't the difference between these two just that in the one case a person could have avoided doing what he did and that in the other case a person could not have avoided getting ill? Doesn't your conception of punishing obliterate this distinction between punishment and treatment?

DANIEL: Yes, that's right. Punishing and treating are exactly the same kind of activities. Neither one presupposes moral responsibility or the ability to have acted differently. Both of them presuppose only that a certain kind of behavior is desirable and that there is a reasonable chance of maintaining it by the punishment or treatment of behavior that deviates from it. Both of these presuppositions are compatible with determinism and the denial of moral responsibility.

FREDERICK: I don't see how you can deny the distinction between punishment and treatment. It is such an essential part of our lives that denying it seems patently false. For example, we put insane people into mental hospitals to be treated, and we put criminals into prisons to be punished. We don't punish insane people, because they can't help doing what they do. We don't even blame them. We just feel pity. But we do punish criminals, because they could have avoided what they did.

DANIEL: The distinction you are referring to is between those kinds of treatment that will deter and change behavior and those that will not. Putting sick persons and insane people into prison will not change their condition, whereas giving them medicine or treating them in mental hospitals will. Putting criminals into prison will deter and change criminal behavior. We call one of these kinds of activities "treating" and the other "punishing," even though neither one presupposes moral responsibility or the ability to act differently.

FREDERICK: But surely there is a difference between being responsible and not being responsible. We commonly suppose that people are responsible for criminal behavior but are not responsible for getting sick. Your denial of moral responsibility obliterates this plain and evident distinction.

DANIEL: I agree with you that there is a distinction between those two cases, but I think it can be accounted for perfectly well by the notion of *causal* responsibility, which is different from *moral* responsibility. We are responsible for criminal behavior because we ourselves cause it, but we are not responsible for getting sick because we do not cause it. We don't need to invoke moral responsibility to explain the difference between these cases.

FREDERICK: Oh yes we do, because causal responsibility is not enough to justify blame and punishment. These are legitimate only if someone has done something wrong.

DANIEL: Again, I agree with you—blaming and punishing make sense only if someone has done something wrong. But just because someone has done something wrong doesn't mean that he is morally responsible for it.

FREDERICK: How can that possibly be so?

DANIEL: Saying that someone has done something wrong is the same as expressing a dislike of it. But disliking something has nothing to do with moral responsibility.

FREDERICK: Can you explain what you mean?

MORALITY

DANIEL: Yes. When people think of morality, they usually think of objective, eternal principles which apply to all people. "It is wrong to torture people just for the fun of it" and "It is better to love than to hate" are two examples. These statements are supposed to express objective truths —they are true regardless of what we like or dislike. In my conception of morality, however, these statements merely express our likes and dislikes. The first one expresses our dislike of torture, and the second expresses our liking of love more than of hate. Neither one expresses an objective, eternal principle which would exist even if people had no likes or dislikes. That's because there are no such principles. There are only likes and dislikes.

FREDERICK: Is that why you think that morality makes sense even though determinism is true, and even though people are not morally responsible for anything they do?

DANIEL: That's right. Our likes and dislikes can exist even though everything we do is caused by happenings over which we have no control.

FREDERICK: Why do you think your conception of morality is correct?

DANIEL: Because it is the conception of morality that best fits in with determinism. It doesn't make sense to say that people have obligations if they cannot avoid doing what they do. But it does make sense to say that people do what other people like or dislike, even though they cannot avoid doing what they do.

FREDERICK: Since your conception of morality seems to conflict with what people usually believe about morality, I would like to ask you a few questions about it.

DANIEL: Okay.

FREDERICK: If you are right in saying that morality is the same as a system of likes and dislikes, then conflicting moral beliefs would be nothing more than differences in what we like. If I say "Wars are always wrong" and someone else says "Wars are sometimes right," we would only be expressing different feelings toward war. We would not be asserting incompatible moral statements—one of which is true and the other of which is false—because truth and falsity do not apply to feelings.

DANIEL: Yes, that's right. On my view of morality, differences in moral beliefs are differences in what we like.

FREDERICK: Well, that goes against our ordinary view of morality, which says that when two people disagree, one of them is right and the other is wrong. So my question is, How can you reconcile your conception of morality with the common belief that people say contradictory things when they disagree about moral matters?

DANIEL: I don't reconcile the two because I reject the common view. We never do say contradictory things when we utter different moral statements. Moral statements that appear to be contradictory are really expressions of different tastes, which are no more contradictory than two people liking different kinds of food.

FREDERICK: But don't people think of themselves as saying something that is true or false when they utter a moral statement such as "He should not have hit him"?

DANIEL: People may think this, but they are wrong if they do, because in actuality they are merely expressing a dislike of one person's having hit another. And dislikes are no more true or false than trees or rivers.

FREDERICK: Suppose someone were to ask you whether or not your likes are good. Would you understand what he was asking?

DANIEL: Yes, certainly.

FREDERICK: Then it follows that morality is something more than mere likes and dislikes. When a person says that his likes are good, he is not merely expressing a like of his own likes. That would be absurd. He is saying something true or false about his own likes.

DANIEL: No, in this case, too, he would be expressing a like. There's nothing absurd in expressing a like of our own likes.

FREDERICK: Don't people directly apprehend moral principles? Don't we all see intuitively that it is wrong to hurt people just for the fun of it?

DANIEL: If we did have special intuitions of moral principles, we would all agree on what is right and wrong. We don't agree, however. So it is hard to escape the conclusion that there aren't any objective moral truths, and that morality is solely a matter of taste.

FREDERICK: How can your conception of morality account for guilt and remorse? Aren't these based on a violation of objective moral laws?

DANIEL: There is no such thing as guilt if you mean by it a violation of objective moral laws. And there is no such thing as remorse if you mean by it a sorrow for having violated an objective moral law. However, there is guilt if it means "not having done what other people would have liked for you to have done"; and there is remorse if it means "sorrow for having done what other people disliked."

FREDERICK: Your answers to my questions show how radical your conception of morality is. They demonstrate the lengths to which a determinist must go just to maintain his belief in determinism. If determinism entails all that, I think it should be rejected.

DANIEL: From my perspective, it is really the other way around. Your rejection of the evidence for determinism, as demonstrated in your remarks near the beginning of our entire discussion on free will and determinism, shows to what lengths a free-willist must go just to maintain his belief in free will. If free will and moral responsibility entail the denial of determinism, I think they should be rejected, no matter what the consequences are for our conception of morality.

FREDERICK: What do you think of all this, Carolyn?

WHETHER DETERMINISM IS COMPATIBLE WITH MORAL RESPONSIBILITY

CAROLYN: I don't think that a person has to say what Daniel has been saying just to maintain his belief in determinism. I think a person can believe in determinism, as I do, without also denying moral responsibility, as Daniel does.

FREDERICK: That certainly is an interesting statement.

CAROLYN: I agree with Daniel that the evidence for determinism is so strong that we have to believe that determinism is true. And I agree with you, Frederick, that the legitimacy of blame, punishment and morality shows that we are morally responsible for what we do. Neither determinism nor moral responsibility can be denied without denying plain and evident facts.

FREDERICK: I take it you believe that moral responsibility is compatible with determinism. Is that correct?

CAROLYN: Yes. A person can believe both without contradicting himself.

FREDERICK: I would like to see you make a case for that, because it seems to me that they are contradictory. Determinism entails that people cannot act differently from the way they actually act, and moral responsibility presupposes that people can act differently from the way they actually act.

CAROLYN: I agree with you that moral responsibility presupposes that people can act differently, but I don't think that this ability to act differently conflicts with determinism. What we mean when we say that we can act differently is that no person or circumstance compels us to act as we do or prevents us from doing something different. And what we do might not be compelled by any person or circumstance even though it is caused by our own beliefs, desires and choices.

FREDERICK: Why do you define the ability to act differently in that way?

CAROLYN: I define the ability to act differently in that way because that is what we normally mean by it. For instance, a bank robber who could have refrained from robbing a bank is one who was not forced to act as he did. A check forger who could have refrained from writing a bad check is one who was not forced to forge another person's signature—and so on. The typical everyday meaning of "being able to act differently" is "not being forced to act as one does or not being prevented from acting differently." It is this typical sense of the ability to act differently which is required by moral responsibility and which is compatible with determinism.

FREDERICK: How exactly is it compatible with determinism?

CAROLYN: Our actions can be caused by our beliefs, desires and choices *and* at the same time be uncompelled by any person or circumstance. The case of the check forger illustrates this nicely. He could have refrained from writing a bad check because no one forced him to do it, yet his doing it was caused by his belief that he could get away with it and by his desire for more money. He was morally responsible for what he did even though his action had a cause.

FREDERICK: You are certainly right in saying that moral responsibility would be compatible with determinism *if* it presupposed only your sense of being able to act differently.

CAROLYN: Do you disagree with me?

FREDERICK: Yes. I think moral responsibility presupposes a different sense of the ability to act differently—a sense that conflicts with determinism.

CAROLYN: Can you explain that sense to me?

FREDERICK: Yes. I think moral responsibility presupposes that we can act differently even if all of the immediately prior conditions are the same. This means that moral responsibility conflicts with determinism, because saying that an occurrence can be different even if all of the immediately prior conditions are the same is identical with saying that the occurrence is uncaused. You explained this when we were discussing the evidence for determinism.

CAROLYN: Yes, that's right.

FREDERICK: Being able to act differently in my sense means that nothing inside or outside a person causes him to act as he does. He can act differently even if everything in his brain, subconscious mind, and external environment is the same. In other words, he has genuine alternatives open to him. If he didn't have genuine alternatives open to him, there would be only one thing he could do—in which case he certainly should not be held morally responsible for what he does.

CAROLYN: Perhaps we should consider a few examples to see exactly what moral responsibility presupposes.

FREDERICK: That's a good idea.

CAROLYN: First, let's take the case of a person who has been caught stealing. If we ask why it is that we think of him as being morally responsible for what he has done, I think the answer is that we assume that he knew he was doing something wrong or at least that he ought to have known he was doing something wrong, and we assume that he was not forced to steal. We don't consider *all* of the immediately prior conditions, as you say we should, because some of them are entirely irrelevant to whether or not he is to be blamed. For instance, we don't even think about what is going on in his brain or subconscious mind. We know he is morally responsible for stealing without having to take him to a neurologist, physiologist and psychiatrist. If you were right in saying that he is morally responsible for stealing only if he can act differently even if *all* of the immediately prior conditions were to remain the same, we would never be able to tell that he is morally responsible for doing what he did. But we know that he is—and that's because moral responsibility presupposes only that he was not compelled to steal, which we can ascertain quite readily.

FREDERICK: It presupposes more than that. If something in the person's brain or subconscious mind caused him to steal, then even though he was not compelled or forced to do what he did, he would, nevertheless, be unable to act any differently from the way he actually acted. And certainly he should not be blamed, punished or held morally accountable for stealing if he could not have done anything else but steal.

CAROLYN: Here's another example. Suppose one night your garage burns down. After investigating, the fire department discovers that it had been set on fire, and several days later the police apprehend the person who did it. Would your indignation be softened if you reflected on the fact that his behavior was determined by a chain of occurrences stretching back prior to his birth, even if you knew that he had deliberately, maliciously and voluntarily set fire to your garage? I think not. What would soften your indignation toward him would be the discovery that he was an otherwise harmless youth who had been goaded and taunted into setting fire to some garage that night by a gang of rowdy toughs.

FREDERICK: If I knew that his action was caused by an endless chain of occurrences, I would not blame him for what he did, because he could not have acted differently.

CAROLYN: Here is one last example. Suppose you were a judge, and a defendant who was accused of assaulting and injuring his neighbor said to you, "Mr. Judge, I am innocent of this charge, because my early childhood experience, upbringing and inherited character traits have all made it such that I could not have acted any differently than I did. Only if something were different in the immediately prior conditions, in my background or in my gene structure could I have avoided assaulting and injuring my neighbor. Therefore, I should not be blamed, punished or held accountable for what I did." What would you think?

FREDERICK: I would think that his defense is just as inappropriate as Clarence Darrow's defense of Leopold and Loeb.

CAROLYN: Why?

FREDERICK: Because although the defendant is right in thinking that he should not be blamed if his crime is determined, he is wrong in assuming that what he did was determined. I don't see how that could possibly be shown.

CAROLYN: I think any judge who reacted in that way would be basing blame, punishment and accountability on an insecure foundation. He would be basing these on the mere hope that our actions could be proven to be uncaused—a hope that has become more and more unfounded as science has provided causal explanations of increasing amounts of human behavior. What we really base blame, punishment and accountability on, as my examples show, is something entirely different. We don't have to investigate the causal history of an action before deciding whether or not we should blame a person for doing it.

FREDERICK: Yes we do. If a person's heredity and early environment make it difficult for him to avoid committing a certain kind of crime, we should soften our blame. For example, a person who has a neurotic impulse to steal probably has had his character molded by circumstances over which he has no control. We shouldn't blame him for what he does, because he can't help it.

CAROLYN: We do sometimes use a person's heredity and early environment as mitigating conditions for blame. But that doesn't mean we should do so *all* of the time. We surely shouldn't refuse to blame the person who deliberately and voluntarily set fire to your garage, even though we can trace the causal history of his action to conditions in his early environment.

FREDERICK: If it is sometimes right to mitigate blame because of a person's heredity or early environment, then it is always right to do so. My robot-person example illustrates this perfectly. You may recall that this example involves an ingenious neurosurgeon who has implanted a device into a certain person's brain. The device causes all of the person's thoughts, desires, choices and actions. Nothing he thinks about, wants to do, chooses and does can be any different from what actually happens. Now let me ask a few questions. Would the robot-person be morally responsible for anything he does? Would we be justified in blaming and punishing him for his misdeeds? Would morality and guilt apply to him? I have asked these questions of people, and invariably I have received a "No" answer. That is because none of the categories we commonly apply to people apply to this robot-person. It makes no sense to say that he should have done one thing rather than another, because he could not have done the other thing. To blame him for doing something illegal is illegitimate, because he is not a moral being. Of course, we might not like what he does and we might want to restrain him from acting in certain ways. But that would not be punishment, because punishment requires that the person punished be a moral agent who has the ability to act differently. And notice, too, that the robot-person fulfills the requirements that you say are necessary for holding someone morally responsible. No one forces him to act as he does, and no one prevents him from acting otherwise, even though the device inside him causes him to do everything he does. This shows, I think, that the sense of "being able to act differently" required by moral responsibility involves something more than not being forced to act as one does. It also involves the ability to act differently, even if everything prior to our action, including what goes on inside us, were to remain the same. This ability is required if we are to have genuine alternatives, which are necessary if blame, punishment, morality and guilt are to apply to people.

CAROLYN: Your example is very persuasive. Unfortunately, its persuasiveness comes from the fact that it neglects entirely our everyday practice of blaming people and making moral judgments about what they do. Our everyday practice ignores the question of whether or not we are all robots. All that it asks is whether or not a person knew what he was doing, and whether or not he was made to do what he did against his will or was prevented from doing something he wanted to do. We all could be robots and still legitimately ask these questions, which means that we all could be robots and still legitimately distinguish between actions for which we are morally responsible and actions for which we are not morally responsible.

FREDERICK: That sounds most paradoxical. If everything we do were caused, I don't see how morality and blame could apply to us. This is shown even more persuasively by my before-birth argument.

CAROLYN: That's the argument you used when we were discussing the compatibility of free will and determinism, right?

FREDERICK: Yes. It says that if determinism were true, everything we do would be caused by a chain of happenings that stretches back to before our births. Since we have no control over what happened prior to our births, we would have no control over what we do now. Everything we do, think, choose and desire would have to be exactly as it is. This means that if determinism were true, we could not be held responsible for anything. Moral obligations would not apply to us, and the distinction between right and wrong would be obliterated.

CAROLYN: My response to that is the same as my response to your robot-person example. We apply blame, punishment and morality in everyday life without regard to what has happened prior to our births. We do not absolve people of moral responsibility when we realize that all of their actions are caused.

FREDERICK: Don't we refuse to apply the distinction between right and wrong to the actions of animals, birds and insects, on the grounds that they are determined to act as they do? Why should it be any different for people, if everything they do is determined?

CAROLYN: The reason we don't apply the distinction between right and wrong to the actions of animals, birds and insects is that they have no knowledge of right and wrong. Whether or not actions are caused has nothing to do with applying moral concepts to the actions.

FREDERICK: But isn't it senseless to say that what we do is right or wrong if it has to be exactly as it is?

CAROLYN: It would be senseless to say that what we do is right or wrong *if* we were forced to act against our wills all the time or were continually prevented from acting as we wish. But we aren't. So right and wrong can apply to our actions even though they are all caused. The causes of our actions—beliefs, desires, choices, brain states, unconscious motives—don't *force* us to act against our wills or prevent us from acting as we wish. People and circumstances do that.

FREDERICK: Isn't it easier to see how people can be morally responsible for their actions if they are uncaused rather than caused?

CAROLYN: No. In fact it is just the reverse. It is easier to see how people can be morally responsible for their actions if they are caused rather than uncaused.

FREDERICK: How can that be so?

CAROLYN: If something we do is uncaused, then, as we have both agreed, it can be different even if all of the immediately prior circumstances were to remain the same. This means that if something we do is uncaused, it can be different even if our beliefs, desires and choices were to remain the same, because these are part of the circumstances that exist immediately prior to our actions. Consequently, uncaused actions would be entirely unconnected to our choices, beliefs and desires. Our actions would be purely arbitrary. We might just as well have done something different, even if we had not chosen to do so or had not believed it to be in our best interests. Now I ask you, how can we be held accountable for actions such as these?

FREDERICK: I am willing to admit that our actions are caused by our beliefs, desires and choices. But that wouldn't remove responsibility from our actions unless the causes were themselves caused by an endless chain of happenings. This is not the case, however, because our actions are the products of our free and uncaused decisions.

CAROLYN: That doesn't answer my argument, because the very same things I just said about actions also apply to uncaused decisions, which you say cause our actions. If a decision is uncaused, it would be entirely unconnected to our character traits and personality patterns. Our making a decision would be purely arbitrary. We might just as well have decided differently, even if nothing in our character or personality were different. How can we be responsible for a decision that is disassociated from ourselves in this way?

FREDERICK: We can be held accountable for uncaused decisions because we are confronted with genuine alternatives when we make them. If our decisions were caused, and the causes caused, and so on, we would not be confronted with genuine alternatives. This makes it easier, for me at least, to see how people can be morally responsible for their decisions if they are uncaused rather than caused.

DANIEL: It doesn't look as if you two are ever going to agree with each other.

Concluding Remarks

CAROLYN: Maybe we should end our discussion of free will and determinism. It's getting rather late.

DANIEL: Have we talked about all of the issues?

FREDERICK: No, but we have talked about some of the important ones.

CAROLYN: We don't seem to have come any closer to agreement. In fact, we seem to have solidified our disagreements.

DANIEL: Since people are continually disagreeing about the answer to the problem, one wonders whether it is possible for anyone ever to know what the right answer is.

FREDERICK: I would say that it is possible. People agree on what general criteria should be used in evaluating the truth of beliefs. And these general criteria can be used in deciding whether determinism is true or whether the free will position is true.

DANIEL: What general criteria do you have in mind?

FREDERICK: A belief has to be in agreement with facts and experiences of every kind; it cannot conflict with other well-established beliefs, and it cannot be self-contradictory.

DANIEL: You are certainly right in saying that people agree to those criteria. But the crucial question is how to apply them. One person might think that his position is true because it conforms to the criteria better than the opposite position. And another person might think that the opposite position is true because *it* conforms to the criteria better than the first position. So how can we tell that a certain position conforms to the criteria better than another position?

FREDERICK: That would be a matter of patiently and carefully examining the evidence.

DANIEL: And when you do that, what do you think is the correct solution to the problem of free will and determinism?

FREDERICK: I think the free will position is correct.

DANIEL: And I think the determinist position is correct.

CAROLYN: It looks as if we'll never settle the issue.

DANIEL: That reminds me of the punishment that the fallen angels received in Milton's *Paradise Lost*, which was to discuss the problem of free will and determinism forever.

FREDERICK: Couldn't they stop?

DANIEL: No. Everything they said was determined.

FREDERICK: That seems absurd. What would be the point of their talking about whether or not people have free will if everything they said was determined?

DANIEL: So they could decide what the truth is.

FREDERICK: But that doesn't make sense if they have no free will.

CAROLYN: Perhaps we should stop our discussion before we get started all over again.

DANIEL: That's a good idea.

CAROLYN: It's been quite enjoyable talking with you two. If you're free sometime, perhaps we can get together again.

DANIEL: I'd be glad to discuss the issue even if we aren't free.

FREDERICK: How can we do that? If we aren't free, then we don't have . . .

CAROLYN: I have to go now. Goodbye, and good luck!

Abstract

INTRODUCTORY REMARKS (p. 1)

In the opening pages, Frederick, Daniel and Carolyn state their positions. Frederick believes that people have free will and concludes that determinism is false. Daniel believes determinism is true and concludes that people have no free will. Carolyn does not believe that determinism and free will conflict; she believes both that determinism is true and that people have free will. She says that she thinks there are three main questions involved in the issue of free will and determinism: 1. Do people have free will? 2. Is determinism true? 3. Are free will and determinism compatible?

DETERMINISM (p. 3)

Carolyn defines "determinism" as "Everything that happens is caused to happen." Daniel wonders why Carolyn doesn't define "determinism" as "People have no control over anything they do." Carolyn explains that the issue of whether or not determinism is true is different from the issue of whether or not people have free will, and is also different from the issue of whether or not determinism conflicts with free will. These issues should be discussed separately, Carolyn says. Frederick agrees that that is a good procedure.

Daniel states that the enormous number of happenings known to have causes justifies the claim that everything that happens has a cause. Both everyday experience and science, he says, provide countless cases of happenings having causes. Carolyn agrees with Daniel's reason for believing determinism. She states this reason in a different way by saying that if a happening has *no* cause, then it could have been different in the way it happened, even if everything just prior to it were exactly the same. Since observation shows that whenever there are differences in the way things usually happen, there are also differences in the prior conditions, we can conclude, Carolyn says, that all happenings have causes. This includes human actions as well as natural events, she says. Frederick responds to Daniel's and Carolyn's arguments for determinism in two ways. His first response is that there is not enough evidence to show that *every* happening is caused. A very small percentage of the world's happenings has been observed, he says, and even the knowledge scientists have about people is general and imprecise. Daniel replies that scientists have found so many causal laws that govern people's behavior that we are justified in inferring that all of our behavior is governed by causal laws. In daily life, he claims, we frequently reason in this way by making inferences from *some* to *all*. Frederick's second response to Daniel's and Carolyn's arguments for determinism is that they ignore the fact that there is actual evidence against determinism. This evidence comes from new discoveries in quantum physics, which has shown, he claims, that the behavior of electrons, photons and other subatomic particles is random and uncaused. Daniel replies that all that quantum physics has really shown is that we don't know the causes of certain kinds of occurrences, not that there are no causes. He states, and Carolyn agrees, that there is no method of observing that an occurrence has no cause. Furthermore, Daniel says, the new discoveries in quantum physics are not relevant to the question of free will, because free actions have not been shown to be the result of uncaused behavior of subatomic particles in our brains.

WHETHER DETERMINISM IS AN EMPIRICAL THEORY (p. 11)

Frederick responds to Daniel's and Carolyn's claim that there is no method of observing that an occurrence has no cause by saying that if this is true, then determinism is not an empirical claim, because a claim that is empirical must be able to be refuted, in principle, by some possible observable circumstance. That means, he says, that Daniel and Carolyn cannot say there is no method of observing that an occurrence has no cause *and* at the same time use empirical evidence to support the truth of determinism. Carolyn replies that in order for a statement to be empirical, it must be either supportable in principle *or* refutable in principle, but it need not be both supportable and refutable in principle. Since "Everything that happens has a cause" is supported by empirical evidence, it is an empirical claim, even though it is not refutable in principle by empirical evidence. Frederick replies that his objection to what Daniel and Carolyn said does not rest on the meaning of the word "empirical," but rests on the claim that if there are observable circumstances which, if they existed, would show determinism to be true, then there should be observable circumstances which, if they existed, would show determinism to be false.

Daniel asserts that there is no way in which we can know that an event does not have a cause, because the most that we can say as limited finite beings is that we have not *found* the cause. And this does not show that an event has no cause, for we might not have looked hard enough or long enough. Frederick wonders, in view of what Daniel says now, whether Daniel really believes that "Every event has a cause" is true on the basis of empirical evidence. Daniel explains that he does not think that "Every event has a cause" is a tautology. Nor does he believe it to be true because of a special insight or intuition he has independently of experience. His reason for thinking that "Every event has a cause" is empirical is that we must observe many events having causes in order to know that it is true. Moreover, if we never or only rarely found the causes of events, Daniel says, then we could say that determinism probably isn't true, although we could never be sure which single events do not have causes. Frederick maintains that unless Daniel can show what possible observations would show that a single event has no cause, he is not justified in thinking that "Every event has a cause" is empirical.

DELIBERATION AND FREE WILL (p. 17)

Carolyn asks Frederick what evidence he uses to try to refute determinism. Frederick argues that the fact that people deliberate about what they are going to do shows that they have free will and that determinism is false. If determinism were true, Frederick claims, then in any given situation a person could not choose differently from the way he actually chooses, since he could choose only what he is determined to choose. But if people deliberate about what they are going to do, then they can choose differently from the way they actually choose. Daniel rejects Frederick's claim about the connection between deliberation and being able to choose differently. It is possible for us to deliberate about what we are going to do, Daniel says, even though our deliberations are caused by happenings over which we have no control. He illustrates his point by giving two examples—one in which an ingenious physiologist causes a person to deliberate, and another in which a hypnotist causes a person to deliberate by means of a posthypnotic suggestion. Frederick does not accept Daniel's illustrations as counterinstances to Frederick's claim. The persons being caused to deliberate by the physiologist and the hypnotist were not really deliberating, because they were not able to choose differently from the way they were caused to choose. Daniel then distinguishes between *actually* being able to choose differently and *thinking* that we are able to choose differently. Deliberation does not presuppose that we are actually able to choose differently, and, therefore, does not presuppose that we have free will and that determinism is false, Daniel says. But if it did entail these things, he would seriously wonder what evidence there is for believing that people ever deliberate. Deliberation presupposes that we think we are able to choose differently, but thinking that we are able to choose differently doesn't show that we are actually able to choose differently.

THE AWARENESS OF FREE WILL (p. 21)

Frederick maintains that the free will position is true because we introspect ourselves acting and choosing freely. We have inner intuitions, he says, of being able to act and choose differently from the way we actually act and choose. Daniel admits that we have such intuitions, but claims that they don't show that we act and choose freely, because intuitions generally are unreliable. Frederick responds by asserting that our intuitions of free will are not like unreliable hunches, because we all have such intuitions. Daniel then claims that it is possible for us to intuit that an action or choice is free even though it is not actually free. That indicates, he says, that our intuitions of free will don't show that we act and choose freely. Frederick retorts that it is possible for us to have perceptions of physical objects even though there are no such objects, so that if Daniel's reasoning were correct, perceptions of physical objects would not show that physical objects exist. Daniel then maintains that the evidence for determinism justifies one in concluding that our intuitions of free will are mistaken. Frederick replies that intuitions of free will are evident and are had by everyone, which means, he says, that they outweigh the evidence for determinism.

WHETHER THE AWARENESS OF FREE WILL CONFLICTS WITH DETERMINISM (p. 26)

Carolyn criticizes Frederick's argument based on intuitions of free will by claiming that our intuitions do not conflict with determinism. When we intuit ourselves acting and choosing freely, Carolyn claims, we do not intuit our actions and choices being able to be different even if everything inside us were to remain the same. We do not have such intuitions because we do not intuit everything going on in our brains and subconscious minds. Yet we would have to have such intuitions, Carolyn says, in order to have intuitions of our actions and choices being uncaused. Frederick replies by giving examples of cases in which we have intuitions of free will. Carolyn says that what we are aware of when we are aware of ourselves acting or deciding freely is that there isn't anything outside us that prohibits us from acting or deciding. This awareness, however, does not conflict with determinism because something inside us might cause us to act or decide as we do.

WHETHER DETERMINISM IS COMPATIBLE WITH FREE WILL (p. 30)

Frederick suggests that the conversation turn to the question of whether determinism is compatible with free will. Carolyn claims that they are compatible. To say that we are free, she says, is to say that there are no persons or external circumstances preventing us from doing what we want to do. Saying that we are free in this sense is compatible with saying that determinism is true, because what we do may be caused by what is inside us, such as brain states and unconscious motives, even though there are no persons or external circumstances preventing us from doing what we want to do. (UNCONSCIOUS, p. 33): Frederick replies that the kind of freedom people would have if Carolyn's compatibilist thesis were true is bogus, for a person could have Carolyn's kind of freedom even though he had no control over anything he did. Frederick illustrates his point with the case of a person who is caused to do everything he does by a device that is implanted in his brain —a person who is nothing more than a robot, yet who has Carolyn's kind of freedom. Carolyn replies that whether or not something inside us causes us to act as we do is irrelevant to whether or not we are free. She says that her view of the nature of human freedom as an absence of external constraints is based on the way the word "free" is ordinarily used, and she wonders what more could be wanted in human freedom than an absence of external constraints. (UNCAUSED, p. 34): Frederick replies that people can have genuine freedom only if their actions and choices are uncaused. This is so, he says, because we have genuine freedom only if we are in control of what we do, and we are in control of what we do only if it is possible for what we do to be different even though everything just prior to what we do were to remain the same. Since this is identical to being uncaused, it follows, says Frederick, that for an action to be free, it must be uncaused, which means that Carolyn cannot say that people are free *and* that determinism is true. (CHANCE, p. 35): Carolyn replies to Frederick's incompatibilist position by challenging Frederick's claim that we are in control of what we do only if what we do is uncaused. Being uncaused is the same as happening as a result of pure chance, Carolyn says, so that if what we do is uncaused, we cannot be in control of it. She illustrates her point by comparing uncaused actions with uncaused electron swerves, which are a clear case of chance phenomena. Frederick replies that there are two differences between a free action and an uncaused electron swerve. A free action is something that a person produces, whereas an electron's swerve is something that happens to the electron. In addition, a free action is usually done for a purpose, whereas an electron's uncaused swerve is not done for a purpose. These differences mean, says Frederick, that uncaused actions are not a result of chance. Carolyn responds by saying that these differences do not remove the element of chance from Frederick's conception of a free action. (BEFORE-BIRTH ARGUMENT, p. 38): Frederick then uses the "before-birth argument" to try to show that Carolyn's compatibilist thesis is mistaken. If determinism is true, then everything a person does is determined by events occurring prior to his birth. Since he has no control over what happened prior to his birth, it follows that if determinism is true, he has no control over anything he does now. Carolyn responds by saying that what happened prior to our births is irrelevant to whether or not we act freely, because we decide whether or not a person acts freely by deciding whether or not there is any person or circumstance preventing him from doing what he wants to do. Carolyn also claims that her concept of freedom is correct because it is linked to other commonly used concepts. Frederick replies that this does not justify Carolyn's concept of freedom and does not refute Frederick's before-birth argument for the incompatibility of free will and determinism. (SUMMARY, p. 40): Daniel, Frederick and Carolyn then summarize their positions.

DETERMINISM AND MORAL RESPONSIBILITY (p. 41)

Frederick then argues that determinism cannot be reconciled with the fact that people are morally responsible for what they do. Determinism and moral responsibility are incompatible, Frederick says, because determinism entails that no one can avoid acting as he does, and moral responsibility presupposes that people can avoid acting as they do. Daniel agrees with Frederick that determinism and moral responsibility are incompatible, but denies that people are ever morally responsible for what they do. Frederick responds by saying that people must be morally responsible for what they do because blame, punishment and morality would make no sense unless people are morally responsible. Daniel replies that blame, punishment and morality do make sense, even though people are not morally responsible for anything they do. (BLAME AND PUNISHMENT, p. 43): This is so, he says, because blame and punishment are used to change people's behavior, to deter people from acting wrongly, and to protect other people from harm. None of these activities presupposes that determinism is false and that people are morally responsible for what they do. Frederick claims that blame and punishment would not be legitimate unless a person could have avoided doing what he did. Daniel denies that this is true on the grounds that the only requirements for the legitimate use of blame and punishment are that the behavior in question be undesirable and that the blaming and punishing be effective in changing behavior, deterring people from doing wrong and protecting people from harm. Frederick says that if blame and punishment do not presuppose that a person could have avoided doing what he did, then there would be no difference between punishing someone for something he has done and treating him for an illness he has. Daniel replies that the only difference between punishment and treatment is that they are used to change different conditions people are in; putting people into prison will not help sick people get well, whereas giving them medicine will. Frederick retorts that punishing is legitimate only if someone has done something wrong. Daniel agrees with this but denies that wrongdoing requires moral responsibility. (MORALITY, p. 46): This is so, he says, because morality is nothing more than a system of likes and dislikes, rather than a system of objective moral laws. Likes and dislikes are compatible with determinism and the denial of moral responsibility, because likes and dislikes do not presuppose an ability to avoid acting as one does. Daniel's reason for adopting this conception of morality is that it is the one that fits in best with determinism. Frederick then asks Daniel several questions about his conception of morality. The questions are: How can Daniel's conception of morality be reconciled with the common belief that people say contradictory things when they disagree about moral matters? Don't people think of themselves as saying something that is true or false when they utter moral statements? When we say "Our likes are good," are we merely expressing a like toward our likes? Don't people directly apprehend moral principles? How can Daniel's conception of morality account for guilt and remorse? Daniel's answers to these questions, Frederick claims, show to what lengths a determinist must go just to maintain his belief in determinism.

WHETHER DETERMINISM IS COMPATIBLE WITH MORAL RESPONSIBILITY (p. 49)

Carolyn claims that moral responsibility does not conflict with determinism, because the kind of ability to act differently that moral responsibility presupposes does not conflict with determinism. To say that a person can do something different from what he actually does, in the sense presupposed by moral responsibility, is to say that no one forces him to do what he does and no one prevents him from doing something different. People can act differently in this sense even though determinism is true, Carolyn says, because their actions can be caused by their beliefs, desires and choices and at the same time be uncompelled by any person or circumstance. She supports her compatibilist contention with three examples—the case of the person caught stealing, the tragedy of the burned garage, and the comedy of the defendant who was an incompatibilist determinist—each of which, she claims, illustrates how the concept of moral responsibility is employed in everyday life. Frederick asserts that the kind of ability to act differently presupposed by moral responsibility includes more than what Carolyn has described. It also includes the ability to act differently, even if all of the immediately prior conditions are the same. Since this is what it means to be uncaused, Frederick concludes that moral responsibility is incompatible with determinism. He supports his position with his robot-person example and with his before-birth argument. Carolyn's response to these is that our everyday practice regarding moral responsibility ignores the question whether or not we are all robots, and ignores the question whether our actions are caused by a chain of events stretching back to before our births. Carolyn then argues that we cannot be morally responsible for uncaused choices, because they are not connected to our character traits or personality patterns. Frederick replies that we are morally responsible for our uncaused choices, because we are confronted with genuine alternatives when we make them.

CONCLUDING REMARKS (p. 56)

The dialogue ends with Daniel wondering whether the correct solution to the problem of free will and determinism can ever be known, with Frederick asserting that it can, and with Carolyn expressing her enjoyment at having discussed the problem with Daniel and Frederick.

Questions

INTRODUCTORY REMARKS (pp. 1–3)

What is your reaction to Darrow's statement?

DETERMINISM (pp. 3–11)

1. Does "determinism" have any connotations that "Every event has a cause" does not have? If so, what?
2. If you were Daniel or Carolyn, how would you answer the following question: How can anyone be justified in believing in determinism if there are many happenings for which causes have not been found?
3. If you were Frederick, how would you answer the following question: In view of the fact that science has found the causes of a great number of happenings, isn't it intellectually irresponsible not to believe in determinism?
4. Do you think the case of the twins with different personalities refutes determinism? Why or why not?
5. Do you think that quantum physics has refuted determinism? If so, how does this refutation relate to the question of whether people have free will?
6. Have Daniel and Carolyn convinced you that determinism is true?

WHETHER DETERMINISM IS AN EMPIRICAL THEORY (pp. 11–17)

1. Do you think Carolyn can satisfactorily answer the following question: How can you maintain that there is no possible way to disprove determinism and yet say that determinism is an empirical claim?
2. Do you think Daniel can satisfactorily answer the following question: Are there any possible observable circumstances which, if they existed, would disprove determinism?
3. Can you think of any way to show that a happening does not have a cause?
4. Can we know that the statement "Everything that happens has a cause" is true by means of a nonempirical insight?
5. Is Daniel right when he says that "there is no way in which we, as limited, finite beings, can know that events don't have causes" (p. 13)?

DELIBERATION AND FREE WILL (pp. 17–21)

1. If you were Daniel, how would you answer the following

question: If a person can think about what he is going to do, doesn't that mean he has free will?

2. If you were Frederick, how would you answer the following question: Why can't a person think about what he is going to do even though what he does is caused by happenings over which he has no control?
3. Do you think Daniel has responded satisfactorily to Frederick's claim that deliberation "involves the ability to choose differently from the way we actually choose" (p. 19)?
4. Do you think Frederick has responded satisfactorily to Daniel's challenge to "prove that we deliberate in a sense that clearly conflicts with determinism" (p. 20)?
5. Do Daniel's two examples (pp. 18–19, 20–21) disprove Frederick's contention that deliberation shows that people have free will?
6. Do you think Frederick can avoid the dilemma Daniel says he is in (p. 21)?

THE AWARENESS OF FREE WILL (pp. 21–26)

1. Do you think Daniel can satisfactorily answer the following question: How can determinism be true if everyone has self-evident intuitions of free will?
2. Do you think Frederick can satisfactorily answer the following question: How can our intuitions of free will show that we actually have free will if our unconscious motives might be causing us to act as we do?
3. Do you think the evidence for free will based on our intuitions of free will outweighs Daniel's and Carolyn's evidence for determinism?
4. Do you think our intuitions of free will are as reliable as our perceptions of physical objects?
5. Does Daniel's illustration of an unfree action which we intuit to be free (p. 24) disprove Frederick's contention that intuitions of free will show that we have free will?

WHETHER THE AWARENESS OF FREE WILL CONFLICTS WITH DETERMINISM (pp. 26–30)

1. If you were Carolyn, how would you respond to the following question: When we intuit ourselves able to act differently from the way we actually act, are we not intuiting something that disproves determinism?
2. If you were Frederick, how would you respond to the fol-

lowing question: How could anyone possibly intuit his actions being uncaused?

3. Do you think Carolyn is right in claiming that we do not ever intuit ourselves able to act differently, even if everything inside us were to remain the same (pp. 27–30)?
4. What exactly are we intuiting when we intuit ourselves acting freely?

WHETHER DETERMINISM IS COMPATIBLE WITH FREE WILL (pp. 30–41)

1. Do you think Carolyn can satisfactorily answer the following two questions: How can people have free will if everything they do is caused by their unconscious minds? How can people have free will if everything they do is caused by happenings occurring prior to their births?
2. Do you think Frederick can satisfactorily answer the following two questions: How can a person's action be in his control if it is uncaused? Doesn't our everyday conception of freedom show that compatibilism is correct?
3. Do you agree with Frederick's claim that Carolyn's conception of freedom is bogus (pp. 33–34)?
4. Do you agree with Carolyn's claim that uncaused actions cannot be free (p. 35)?
5. Do you think Frederick's before-birth argument for the incompatibility of free will and determinism is sound?
6. Do you agree with Carolyn's compatibilism?

DETERMINISM AND MORAL RESPONSIBILITY (pp. 41–49)

1. If you were a determinist, would you deny that people are morally responsible for what they do, as Daniel does, or would you try to reconcile moral responsibility with determinism, as Carolyn does? Why?
2. Would blame and punishment make sense if people were not morally responsible for what they do, as Daniel claims?
3. Do you think Daniel can satisfactorily answer the following question: How can you distinguish between punishment and treatment if no one is morally responsible for anything?
4. If you had to choose between determinism and objective morality, which would you choose? Can a person consistently believe both?

WHETHER DETERMINISM IS COMPATIBLE WITH MORAL RESPONSIBILITY (pp. 49–56)

1. Do you think Carolyn's three examples support her conten-

tion that moral responsibility is compatible with determinism?

2. Do you think Frederick's robot-person example and before-birth argument support his contention that moral responsibility is incompatible with determinism?
3. Can human actions be right or wrong if they are all determined?
4. If you were Frederick, how would you respond to the following question: How can we be responsible for uncaused actions—actions that are unconnected to our characters?
5. If you were Carolyn, how would you respond to the following question: How can we be responsible for actions that are a product of happenings over which we have no control?

CONCLUDING REMARKS (pp. 56–58)

Can the correct solution of the problem of free will and determinism be known? If so, how? If not, why not?

Additional Questions

1. If a person believes both that determinism is true and that God made the world, then he also seems committed to believing that God is ultimately responsible for all the pain, suffering and moral evil in the world. Can such a person also believe that God is perfectly good? Must he adopt the free will position in order to reconcile his belief in a perfectly good God with the existence of pain, suffering and moral evil?
2. If determinism is true, then everything that happens seems necessary, including all of the world's pain, suffering and moral evil. Thus, if determinism is true, the world seems necessarily bad, as opposed to contingently bad. How can a determinist reconcile this apparent consequence of determinism with the deep and widespread conviction that evil is not a necessary feature of the world?
3. Must a determinist be a materialist? Can he believe that people possess nonmaterial souls?
4. Can a determinist believe that there is life after death?
5. Must a determinist be an atheist?
6. If determinism is true, then we seem to be nothing more than mere pawns who are pushed about by a mechanistic and unconscious nature. And if theism is true, then we would seem to be nothing more than puppets whose every move is controlled by God. Can life have meaning if either of these is true? Must a person adopt the free will position

in order to believe that life has meaning?

7. If determinism is true, then all of our beliefs are caused. And if that is so, it would seem that we cannot help but have the beliefs we do have. Can the determinist reconcile this apparent consequence of his position with the fact that we choose our beliefs on the basis of what we think are good reasons?
8. Can you think of any other solution to the problem of free will and determinism than those proposed by Daniel, Frederick, and Carolyn?

Suggested Readings

I. Introductory Treatments

Cornman, James W., Lehrer, Keith and Pappas, George S. "The Problem of Freedom and Determinism." In *Philosophical Problems and Arguments: An Introduction,* 4th ed. Indianapolis: Hackett Publishing Company, 1992.

Hospers, Lohn. "The Casual Principle," "Determinism and Freedom." In *An Introduction to Philosophical Analysis,* 4th ed. Englewood Cliffs, N. J. : Prentice-Hall, 1996.

Taylor, Richard. "Freedom and Determinism." In *Metaphysics.* 4th ed. Englewood Cliffs, N. J. : Prentice-Hall, 1992.

——. "Determinism." In *The Encyclopedia of Philosophy,* edited by Paul Edwards. New York: Macmillan and FreePress, 1967.

II. Anthologies

Berofsky, Bernard, ed. *Free Will and Determinism.* New York: Harper, 1966.

Dworkin, Gerald, ed. *Determinism, Free Will and Moral Responsibility.* Englewood Cliffs, N. J. : Prentice-Hall, 1970.

Enteman, Willard F., ed. *The Problem of Free Will: Selected Readings.* New York: Scribner's, 1967.

Hook, Sidney, ed. *Determinism and Freedom In the Age of Modern Science.* New York: Collier, 1961.

Lehrer, Keith, ed. *Freedom and Determinism.* New York: Random House, 1966.

Pereboom, ed. *Free Will.* Indianapolis: Hackett Publishing Company, 1997

Morris, Herbert, ed. *Freedom and Responsibility: Readings in Philosophy and Law.* Stanford, Calif.: Stanford University Press, 1961.

The following anthologies contain valuable selections on free will and determinism:

Blackstone, William, T., ed. *Meaning and Existence: Introductory Readings In Philosophy.* New York: Holt, Rinehart and Winston, 1971.

Edwards, Paul, and Pap, Arthur, eds.. *A Modern Introduction to Philosophy.* 3rd ed. New York: Free Press, 1973.

Feinberg, Joel and Shafer-Landau, Russ, eds.. *Reason and Responsibility.* 10th ed. Belmont, Calif.: Wadsworth, 1998.

III. Books

Adler, Mortimer J. *The Idea of Freedom.* Garden City, N.Y.: Doubleday, 2 vols., 1958 and 1961.

Campbell, C. A. *In Defence of Free Will.* London: George Allen and Unwin, 1967.

Darrow, Clarence. *Crime: Its Cause and Treatment.* New York: Crowell, 1922.

Edwards, Jonathan. *Freedom of the Will.* Edited by Paul Ramsey. New Haven: Yale University Press, 1957.

Lamont, Corliss. *Freedom of Choice Affirmed.* New York: Horizon Press, 1983.

Young, Robert. *Freedom, Responsibility and God.* New York: Harper, 1975.

IV. Articles and Chapters in Books

BonJour, Laurence A. "Determinism, Libertarianism, and Agent Causation." *The Southern Journal of Philosophy* 14 (Summer 1976): 145-156.

Broad, C. D. "Determinism, Indeterminism, and Libertarianism.: In *Ethics and the History of Philosophy.* London: Routledge and Kegan Paul, 1952. Reprinted in Berofsky and Dworkin.

Darrow, Clarence. "From the Plea in Defense of Loeb and Leopold." Clarence Darrow and Wallace Rice, eds. *Infidels and Heretics.* Boston: Stratford, 1929.

Edwards, Rem B. "Is Choice Determined by the 'Strongest Motive'?" *American Philosophical Quarterly* 4 (January 1967): 72-78.

Ferré, Fredrick. "Self-Determinism." *American Philosophical Quarterly* 10 (July 1973): 165-176.

Frank, Philipp. "The New Language of the Atomic World," "Metaphysical Interpretations of the Atomic World." In *Philosophy of Science.* Englewood Cliffs, N. J.: Prentice-Hall, 1957.

Ginet, Carl. "Can the Will Be Caused?" *The Philosophical Review* 71 (January 1962): 49–55.

Grünbaum, Adolf. "Free Will and Laws of Human Behavior." *American Philosophical Quarterly* 8 (October 1971): 299–317.

James, William. "The Dilemma of Determinism." In *The Will to Believe*. New York: Longmans, Green and Co., 1897. Reprinted in Blackstone, Edwards and Pap, and Enteman.

Lehrer, Keith. "Can We Know That We Have Free Will by Introspection?" *The Journal of Philosophy* 57 (March 1960): 145–156.

MacIntyre, A. C. "Determinism." *Mind* 66 (January 1957): 28–41. Reprinted in Berofsky.

Mandelbaum, Maurice. "Determinism and Moral Responsibility." *Ethics* 70 (April 1960): 204–219.

Margenau, Henry. "Quantum Mechanics, Free Will and Determinism." *The Journal of Philosophy* 64 (November 9, 1967): 714–725.

Nowell-Smith, P. H. "Freedom and Responsibility (1) and (2)." In *Ethics*. London: Penguin Books, 1954.

Rée, Paul. "Determinism and the Illusion of Moral Responsibility." Paul Edwards and Arthur Pap, eds. *A Modern Introduction to Philosophy*. 3rd ed. New York: Free Press, 1973, 10–27.

Taylor, Richard. "Deliberation and Foreknowledge." *American Philosophical Quarterly* 1 (January 1964): 73–80. Reprinted in Berofsky.

Taylor, Richard. "Fatalism." *The Philosophical Review* 71 (January 1962): 56–66.

Warnock, G. J. "Every Event Has a Cause." Antony Flew, ed. *Logic and Language*, Second Series. Oxford: Blackwell, 1955.

V. Bibliographies

Many of the items in I, II, and III contain useful bibliographies. An extensive annotated bibliography, with items grouped according to topic, is contained in Paul Edwards and Arthur Pap, eds., *A Modern Introduction to Philosophy*, 3rd ed., New York: Free Press, 1973, 99–114. *The Philosopher's Index* (published quarterly) lists and summarizes current articles.

Index